BRITAIN

A Rand McNally Pocket Guide

Nicole Swengley

Rand McNally & Company
Chicago   New York   San Francisco

The author wishes to express thanks to
the following organizations for help in compiling material:
British Tourist Authority,
English, Scottish and Wales Tourist Boards,
Regional Tourist Boards, Automobile Association.

Cover photographs
British Tourist Authority:
Pass of Killiecrankie, Lincoln Cathedral, Llangollen
J. Allan Cash: Chatsworth House, Derbyshire
Van Phillips: Trooping the Colour, London
Tony Ridge: St Ives, Cornwall

Photographs
Peter Baker
pp. 38, 46, 53, 55(bottom), 63(top), 71, 79(right), 85(top), 97(top), 105, 106

British Tourist Authority
pp. 39(right), 45, 84, 123(top left)

J. Allan Cash
pp. 29, 39(left), 65, 78, 79(left), 90, 97(bottom), 103(top), 115

Keith Ellis
p. 28(right)

Van Phillips
pp. 28(left), 34, 72, 103(bottom)

Tony Ridge
pp. 122(mid right; bottom), 123(bottom), 124

Scottish Tourist Board
pp. 113, 122(top left and right; mid left), 123(top right; mid left)

Zefa
pp. 55(top), 56, 63(bottom), 73(top), 85(bottom), 95

Town Plans
M. and R. Piggott

Illustration
pp. 6–7 Peter Joyce

HOW TO USE THIS BOOK

The contents page of this book shows how the country is divided up into tourist regions. The book is in two sections: general information and gazetteer. The latter is arranged in the tourist regions with an introduction and a regional map (detail below left). All main entries listed in the gazetteer are shown on the regional maps, (distances given within gazetteer entries are approximate). There are also plans of the three capital cities (detail below right): London, Cardiff and Edinburgh; places to visit and leisure facilities available in each city are indicated by symbols. Main roads and railways are shown on the maps and plans.

Regional Maps

〜〜〜 river

········· canal

⬭ lake/reservoir

▲ 884 spot height (feet)

—·—·—·— national boundary

—··—··— county/region boundary

············ national park boundary

═══◯═══ motorway

══════ main road

———— railway

⊕ main airport

✈ other airport

⬡ major built-up area

▨ ◉ ◎ ◦ • city/town/village (in order of size)

metres	feet
1000	3281
500	1640
200	656
100	328
0 land dep.	0 land dep.

0 10 20 30 40 kms
0 5 10 15 20 25 miles

Town Maps

🏰 castle/fortress

⌗ interesting building

✝ religious building

▣ museum

m monument

POL police station

ℹ information centre

✉ post office

✸ town hall

📖 library

▣ theatre

❊ garden

● railway station

🚌 bus terminal

⊖ underground station

Ⓟ car park

Every effort has been made to give you an up-to-date text but changes are constantly occurring and we will be grateful for any information about changes you may notice while travelling.

CONTENTS

Regions, Counties and Islands

BRITAIN

England, Scotland and Wales – these are the constituent parts of Britain with which we deal in this book, and, although the Isle of Man and Channel Islands do not strictly belong to the United Kingdom but are dependencies of the Crown, we have included them for interest's sake. Northern Ireland, part of the United Kingdom, is included in the guide to Ireland in this series and is not mentioned here.

One of Britain's main advantages for visitors is its size – only 1120km/700mi north–south by 480km/300mi east–west. A compact area indeed, with England comprising 130,367sq km/50,335sq mi; Scotland 78,772sq km/30,414sq mi; Wales 20,764sq km/8011sq mi. Even a brief stay can provide sufficient time to sample Britain's varied landscapes and discover some of its myriad attractions, due to the comparatively short travelling time between places. Yet the golden rule is: take your time. Go too fast and you'll miss the many surprises – prehistoric and Roman remains, Norman castles and ruined abbeys, cathedrals and historic houses.

You'll need to bring warm clothes (even in summer) and a waterproof coat. Although the climate is on the whole temperate and mild with prevailing winds from the south west, the weather is very changeable and differs from place to place. (Telephone numbers for regional weather forecasts are given at the front of each area's telephone directory.)

Britain's landscape encompasses moors and mountains, lakes and hills, forests, meadows and sandy beaches. Much natural beauty has been preserved, although it's best to visit the more famous parts such as the Lake District and West Country in spring and autumn to avoid most of the crowds. Flora and fauna are as diverse as Britain's physical features and are mentioned in the regional sections of the gazetteer.

The history of Britain, the character of its people, their attitudes, institutions and manners have been shaped by the island's geographical position on the north-west fringe of the continent of Europe. The country is made up of 54·2 million people and their temperament varies as much as their ancestry. Celts, Saxons, Angles, Jutes, Danes, Normans, Irish, Scots, Welsh, Flemings, Huguenots, Jews, Africans, West Indians and Indians are among the races which have contributed their own particular traits to the British character.

'Typical' British qualities are held to be reliability, honesty, calmness combined with a readiness to handle emergencies. In general, Welsh people tend to be more serious and sensitive than their English counterparts who have a highly developed sense of humour with a penchant for jokes based on understatement. North of the Midlands, folk are regarded as harder working, tougher and more direct. Although the British are generally optimistic, running down Britain is a national pastime – but one which may be indulged only if you are yourself British! The Victorian notion that difficulties are sent to 'bring out the best' is still upheld.

The British queue for everything and courtesy is revered and occasionally practised – few travellers now surrender their seat to a woman or elderly person but all consider it polite to do so. Belief in an individual's right to choose his/her own way of life is a venerated concept and freedom of speech is part of this tradition – you have only to visit Speaker's Corner in London's Hyde Park to witness this.

Concealing eccentricity beneath a deceptively reserved exterior, this race of individualists covets the qualities best seen in their choice of heroes in fact and fiction. The underdog is applauded; bravery, determination, wit and chivalry are admired, particularly in the struggle to defend a personal code of honour against evil forces. Alfred the Great and Robert the Bruce both fought to expel invaders; Robin Hood outwitted bad King John; Sir Francis Drake defeated the Spanish Armada for sake of Queen and country; Sherlock Holmes strove for justice; even highwayman Dick Turpin is condoned because of his flamboyance and inventiveness. Affection for the underdog is equalled only in Britain by fondness for the dog and other domestic pets.

An increased amount of leisure time has enabled many people to pursue hobbies like painting, pottery, music, car mainten-

ance and attending non-vocational courses. Weekends are spent gardening (home ownership with one's own front door and garden is a British priority), home decorating, watching television and video films, reading, playing musical instruments or board/card games and entertaining friends. The British are enthusiastic about sport, particularly football (soccer), rugby, cricket, golf, tennis, athletics, showjumping and horse racing. Other spare-time activities include visiting pubs (public houses), theatres and cinemas, clubs, discos and dance-halls, and playing bingo. The post-war economic boom enabled the standard of living to be improved dramatically and this has, on the whole, been maintained despite current economic problems, while new freedoms in society, indicated by dress and habit, have had a levelling effect on the old class structure.

Britain imports much of its food and raw materials while exporting manufactured goods – machinery, cars, chemicals, woollen and synthetic textiles, drugs, whisky, electrical equipment. Although older industries are increasingly making way for services like tourism, established occupations like mining (coal, ores, North Sea oil and gas) fishing and agriculture (stock-rearing, dairy and arable, vegetable, fruit) are all still important.

Britain has had a continuous monarchy since 802 (except for the Cromwellian period, 1649–60). The Head of State is Her Majesty Queen Elizabeth II, Head of Commonwealth and Defender of the Faith. But whereas the sovereign once had overall power, she is now said to 'reign but not rule' and the country is run by Her Majesty's Government in the name of the Queen.

British Parliament comprises the House of Lords (upper chamber composed of peers of the realm) and House of Commons (lower chamber); the latter is the real seat of power and is elected by British citizens of 18 years and over. After a General Election, the political party with the majority of members in the House of Commons forms the Government. The leader of that party becomes Prime Minister and chooses senior members to form the Cabinet which initiates government policy. The Civil Service and Local Government are responsible for carrying out this policy within administrative areas based on the various counties and regions into which Britain is partitioned.

These same counties and regions make up the 'tourist' areas used in this book to introduce the distinctive regional identities which comprise Britain: the city of **London**; within easy reach of the capital, the resorts of the **South East**; the **South**, including the Isle of Wight and the Channel Islands; full of legend and the most popular tourist area in England, the **West Country**; the compact and highly individual principality of **Wales**; the essential Englishness at the **Heart of England**; not far from London, downlands and river settings of the **Thames and Chilterns**; the fenland and tranquil Constable country of **East Anglia**; at the centre, the **Shires**, made up of the counties of Derby, Leicester, Lincoln, Northampton and Nottingham; moving north, the **Rose Counties** with moors, peaks, dales, seaside resorts and the historic Isle of Man; the **North**, magnificent country which includes the Lake District; across the Border, the **Lowlands** of Scotland with pastoral scenery and Edinburgh, one of Europe's great capitals; **Highlands and Islands** rugged and dramatic, one of the most beautiful regions in the world.

THE PAST

Prehistoric cairns and long barrows (burial mounds) are among the remaining relics of early man's presence in Britain, a presence interrupted, from 700 BC onwards, by successive waves of invading Celtic tribes from Europe, who introduced their knowledge of the working of iron into the country.

A later invader, Julius Caesar, came twice to Britain in 55 BC and 54 BC but withdrew each time leaving the Roman conquest to begin in earnest under Claudius in AD 43. Roman occupation is still conspicuous in fortifications like Hadrian's Wall, erected to keep out warmongering northern tribes, and in towns like London, the heart of their communications network, Colchester, Bath and Caerleon in south-east Wales.

The Roman retreat, from AD 410, left Britain free for further invasion, this time by groups of Angles, Saxons and Jutes from Europe and the Baltic area, while, from 856 onwards, the Vikings swept across the North Sea from Denmark to plunder Britain's monasteries which had begun to flourish with the spread of Christianity. Despite resistance from Alfred the Great (871–99), who controlled the southern Saxon-dominated area, they settled in around the north east calling their territory 'Danelaw'. Alfred's son, Edward the Elder (899–924) reclaimed the Danelaw and, although he let the Danes administer that area, he united north and south to become England's first true king.

The English crown continued to grace the heads of Saxons and Danes until William the Conqueror defeated Harold II at the Battle of Hastings, in 1066, bringing French influence to bear on Britain. William ordered a detailed survey of his newly-won country and his Domesday Book, the record of this survey (1086), is displayed in London's Public Record Office. Castle and abbey building was another Norman pastime, which still remains much in evidence throughout Britain.

While Scotland was ruled by its own line of kings and queens and Wales by its sovereign princes, England's monarchs battled continually with the barons (landowners) and the Roman Church, which had been made supreme in England by the Synod of Whitby (664). Finally, in 1215, King John was forced to bow to his barons and sign the Magna Carta (Great Charter) which restricted the king's power. In 1265, during the reign of Henry III, Simon de Montfort, powerful Earl of Leicester, held a parliament which made constitutional history by admitting a number of common folk (representatives from the towns) to sit with members of the aristocracy. This assembly contained the seed of the present parliamentary system.

In architecture, the transition from Norman to Early Gothic began in the late 12th century, with Early Gothic seen at its finest in Wells and Salisbury Cathedrals. It continued throughout the 13th century, the latter part of which witnessed Edward I's building programme of fortified towns and castles in Wales.

England's relationship with both Wales and Scotland was an uneasy one. Edward I conquered Wales in 1283, but Scotland ensured its own independence at the Battle of Bannockburn, 1314. France continued to exercise an influence on Britain, particularly as Edward III's claim to the French throne, in 1337, sparked off the Hundred Years' War with France. The French side was finally overcome by Henry V at the Battle of Agincourt, 1415.

The Wars of the Roses raged in England from 1455, with the Houses of York and Lancaster fighting for the right

to rule. In 1485, however, Henry Tudor, Lancastrian claimant to the throne, defeated Richard III at the Battle of Bosworth and became King Henry VII, thus bringing a Welsh house to the English throne (Henry V's widow had married Henry VII's grandfather, a Welsh knight). Henry VIII finally joined England and Wales by the Statute of Union, 1536. He also abolished Papal authority in England, dissolved the monasteries, established the Church of England with himself at its head as Defender of the Faith, and married six wives.

The stability of Henry VIII's rule diminished the need for fortified houses and Tudor architecture produced fine manor houses which gradually flowered into stately Elizabethan and Jacobean residences, many of which can still be seen today.

Henry VIII was also responsible for the expansion of the navy, and his able daughter, Elizabeth I, encouraged sea-going trade, particularly the discovery of new routes, markets and products. Elizabeth's reign (1558–1603) was also marked by a flourishing of the arts – Shakespeare was writing then. Her last skilful political move was to leave her throne to 'our cousin Scotland' – James VI, a Stuart, who also became James I of England in 1603, thus uniting the two countries' crowns, although Scotland kept its own government for another century.

The Stuart dynasty's insistence on absolutism led to civil war (1642–5) between the Cavaliers (Royalists) and Roundheads (Puritans) and resulted in the beheading of Charles I in 1649 and the creation by Oliver Cromwell, the leading Puritan, of a republic. Cromwell established a Protectorate which he ruled as Lord Protector, 1653–8. His son, Richard, succeeded him but resigned in 1659.

The monarchy was restored with Charles II (1660–85) and during Queen Anne's reign (1702–14) the Scottish Parliament signed away its separate existence, in 1707, in the Act of Union which united it with the English Parliament.

Trade prospered throughout the years despite troubles with Scotland (Highlanders rebelled against the Union, in 1715 and 1745) and France (Seven Years' War began in 1756). By the end of Anne's reign, Britain had become the world's most important commercial nation, trading with America, Europe and the Orient. Perhaps as a symbol of increasing self-confidence, Georgian architecture (1702–1837) began to dominate English taste with solid Palladian mansions set in parks – frequently landscaped by Capability Brown and enlivened by follies (mock castles or temples, built to satisfy an often eccentric fancy), lakes and gazebos. Gradually, not only houses but whole streets, squares and towns were built in the distinctive Georgian style and many examples remain today, notably in Bath, Edinburgh and London.

Joint rule of Britain and the German state of Hanover had been established with the accession of George I in 1714. During the sovereignty of the four successive Georges, an empire was founded in India while, due to the muddled policies of George III, the War of American Independence (1775–83) enabled George Washington to establish an independent republic in a former colony. The wars against the French, led by Napoleon, culminated successfully for Britain at the Battle of Waterloo in 1815.

Events at home included the Abolition of Slave Trade (1807); opening of the Stockton-Darlington railway (1825); the founding of Trade Unions, and widening of the electorate through the Reform Bill (1832) and the passing of the Factory Acts (1833 onwards) to regulate conditions and hours of work.

Combined rule of Britain and Hanover ceased with Queen Victoria's accession, and her long reign (1837–1901) coincided with a period of prosperity as the country shook off its agricultural bias and emerged as an economy based mainly on industry. The British Empire, largest in world history, was at its height then and Britain's self-assurance expressed itself at home in a confident mode of architecture: Greek and Gothic Revival.

World Wars dominate 20th-century history, the first, 1914–18, in George V's reign, the second, 1939–45, during the reign of George VI. Between the wars, The Statute of Westminster (1931) established the Commonwealth of Nations and marked the end of the British Empire. India achieved independence in 1947 and, in the years following, many former colonies received independence. Britain's present Queen, Elizabeth II, succeeded to the throne in 1952. Britain joined the European Economic Community (Common Market) in 1973.

THE ARTS

Britain is a particularly literary nation. There have been leading scientists, musical composers, painters, inventors and architects, but it is in literature above all that the British excel.

Britain's literary tradition stretches back beyond the jewelled poetry and prose of Anglo-Saxon days, with each subsequent century spawning new writers whose contributions have been of world importance.

The 14th and 15th centuries were dominated by Geoffrey Chaucer, chronicler of *The Canterbury Tales* and by Sir Thomas Malory whose *Morte D'Arthur* anticipated the British proclivity for hero figures – in this case King Arthur; much later, Ian Fleming's spy-hero James Bond. The 16th and 17th centuries produced great playwrights as well as poets. William Shakespeare, who combined both talents, has long been regarded as Britain's unsurpassed literary lion. Other works to reckon with include plays by Christopher Marlowe and Ben Jonson, the hellfire sermons and poetry of John Donne, and John Milton's epic poem *Paradise Lost.*

The 18th century gave birth to diverse styles of creative expression, such as the celebrated diaries of Samuel Pepys and Daniel Defoe's novel *Robinson Crusoe*, one of the forerunners of the genre. The satire of Jonathan Swift, author of *Gulliver's Travels* and of the poet Alexander Pope, the histories of Edward Gibbon, and the essays of Dr Samuel Johnson (who compiled England's most famous dictionary) are among the various techniques which developed alongside the more traditional skills practised in the plays of Goldsmith and Sheridan.

The poetry of Robert Burns (Scotland's national poet), William Wordsworth and poet/painter William Blake spanned the 18th and 19th centuries, followed by the unparalleled verse of Lord Byron, Shelley, Keats, Gerard Manley Hopkins and Tennyson. The novel evolved under the pens of Charles Dickens, Thomas Hardy and the Scottish writer, Sir Walter Scott, while new ground was broken by Jane Austen, George Eliot and the Brontë sisters. Matthew Arnold, novelist Anthony Trollope, playwrights Oscar Wilde and George Bernard Shaw also played starring roles on the populous 19th-century literary stage.

Names to conjure with in the 20th century include H.G. Wells, J.B. Priestley, Bertrand Russell, Somerset Maugham, Virginia Woolf, D.H. Lawrence, Aldous Huxley, Welsh poets W.H. Davies and Dylan Thomas, T.S. Eliot (American, but English by adoption), Christopher Fry and George Orwell.

Of course there are too many to name, so if you are especially interested in visiting Britain's literary shrines, an excellent companion is *The Oxford Literary Guide to the British Isles* edited by Dorothy Eagle and Hilary Carnell.

British people have the same high regard for invention as for literature, and a new era in scientific tradition came about with the onset of the Industrial Revolution, when invention was put to practical use. Much of Britain's industrial development was made possible by Stephenson's pioneering of the steam locomotive, and with the improvement in communications – canals, railroads, bridges – came trade and prosperity. But British ingenuity can be seen throughout history – from Isaac Newton's Law of Gravity formulated in the 17th century, Michael Faraday's discovery of electro-magnetic induction (1831) and Charles Darwin's theory of evolution in his controversial *Origin of Species* (1859) to the Scottish engineer John Logie Baird's creation of the first public TV picture (1929). Britain has had 'firsts' in many areas – medicine, physics, electronics, aeronautics and engineering – which have led to innovations like the hovercraft, invented by Christopher Cockerell, and the first supersonic airliners.

Although painting has a long tradition in Britain, architecture, whose leading exponents included Christopher Wren and Inigo Jones, was the dominant visual art until the end of the 18th century. Even when international artistic recognition was accorded to William Hogarth's satirical engravings and portraits by Sir Joshua Reynolds, attention at home was still focused on the three-dimensional form – demonstrated so admirably in the work of Robert Adam, Scottish architect, who not only built houses but furnished them too.

Successful portrait painters, Thomas Gainsborough and George Romney, were followed by acclaimed landscape artists J.M.W. Turner and John Constable. The 19th-century Pre-Raphaelite Brotherhood was a group of painters and writers, which included London-born Dante Gabriel Rossetti, William Holman Hunt and John Millais. William Morris was a brilliant all-rounder, admired as much for his writing as for his ability in design.

Universally acknowledged 20th-century artists include Augustus John, Francis Bacon, Stanley Spencer and Graham Sutherland, while significant sculptors, like Jacob Epstein, Henry Moore and Barbara Hepworth, also emerged.

As for music, Britain boasts only a handful of indigenous composers – 17th-century Purcell, 18th-century Handel (who came from Bavaria) and perhaps most 'typically' British, Edward Elgar and Vaughan Williams. Gilbert and Sullivan (words and music, respectively) produced a glittering string of 19th-century operettas, such as *The Mikado*, while the 20th

century has pricked up its ears to film music by Walton and operas by Benjamin Britten. The popular music of the 'Swinging Sixties' created its own ephemeral culture. Initially inspired by songs composed and sung by The Beatles and similar pop groups, it also influenced contemporary poetry and alternative art forms – magazines, fashion and design.

PAPERWORK

Passports Entry requirements vary according to your nationality. Generally, the rule is: if you are a citizen of Belgium, France, Federal Republic of Germany, Italy or Luxembourg, you must present a National Identity Card or Passport; Netherlands, you must present a Toeristenkaart or Passport; Austria, Liechtenstein, Monaco or Switzerland, you must present a National Identity Card and Visitors Card (for visits of up to six months) and a Passport (over six months). Citizens of all other countries, including British Commonwealth countries must present a Passport. (If you lose your passport in Britain, notify local police and your own consulate immediately.) **US Citizens** Passports are valid for ten years. Apply to your nearest Passport Agency (check in local telephone book under 'US Government, Department of State', or call at local post office). If this is your first US passport, or if your current passport is over eight years old, you must apply in person; otherwise apply by mail. You must send a completed application form, proof of US citizenship (birth certificate), identification (such as driver's licence) and two recent identical photographs, plus fee. Further information from your local Passport Agency, or write to: Office of Passport Services, Dept. of State, Washington DC 20524. **Canadian Citizens** Passports are valid for five years. Apply by mail with application forms from your local post office to: Passport Office, Dept. of External Affairs, 125 Sussex Drive, Ottawa, Ontario K1A 0G3, or in person at regional passport offices in Vancouver, Edmonton, Winnipeg, Toronto, Montreal, Halifax, Hamilton, Quebec City, Saskatoon, St John's Newfoundland. Documentation required as for US (above). **EEC Citizens** Only an Identity Card is needed for entry.
Visas A current visa, obtainable in advance of arrival from your nearest British official representative, is also required for citizens of African countries (except Algeria, Ivory Coast, Morocco, Nigeria, Tunisia and Republic of South Africa), Albania, Asian countries (except Bahrain,

Israel, Japan, Kuwait, Maldive Islands, Republic of Korea, Qatar, Turkey and United Arab Emirates), the Argentine Republic, Bulgaria, Cuba, Czechoslovakia, German Democratic Republic, Hungary, Poland, Romania and the USSR.

Vaccinations Requirements can vary, but it is unlikely that you will be required to have an International Certificate of Vaccination. You are advised to check with local health authorities whether a vaccination certificate is needed on re-entry into your own country.

Insurance

Before arrival in Britain, check that your insurance policy covers accidents and illness abroad. You should have adequate insurance to cover cancellation charges, medical expenses and third person or public liability abroad, baggage loss or theft, and repatriation in case of accident, illness or family crisis. Those planning a sporting holiday, including casual swimming, should make sure all activities are covered. Inexpensive short-term insurance can easily be obtained through a travel agent or insurance broker. Your policy will explain claim procedure. **Car**

users see p. 15 for necessary car documentation and insurance. **EEC Citizens** See p. 23 for availability of reciprocal health arrangements between EEC countries.

Customs and Excise

A red and green Clearway System is in operation at most ports and airports in Britain. Go through the Red Channel if you have goods to declare, or the Green Channel, subject to spot-checks by a Customs Officer, if you have nothing to declare.

What you must declare Alcoholic drinks, tobacco goods, perfume, toilet water and any articles over the duty- and tax-free allowances shown in the table below, plus any prohibited or restricted goods. If duty is due, it must normally be paid before leaving the Customs Hall. Persons under 17 are not entitled to the tobacco and alcohol allowances.

Prohibited and restricted goods Don't try to import illegally any prohibited or restricted goods such as controlled drugs; counterfeit coins; gold coins, medals, medallions and similar gold pieces; firearms; ammunition and explosives; flick knives; horror comics; indecent

Duty-free allowances *subject to change*		Goods bought in a duty-free shop	Goods bought in EEC
Tobacco	Cigarettes or	200	300
Double if you live outside Europe	Cigars *small* or	100	150
	Cigars *large* or	50	75
	Pipe tobacco	250 gm	400 gm
Alcohol	Spirits *over 38.8° proof* or	1 litre	1½ litres
	Fortified or sparkling wine plus	2 litres	3 litres
	Table wine	2 litres	5 litres
Perfume		50 gm	75 gm
Toilet water		250 cc	375 cc
Other goods		£28	£210

US customs permit duty-free $300 retail value of purchases per person, 1 quart of liquor per person over 21, and 100 cigars per person.

and obscene books, magazines, films; meat and poultry (uncooked); radio telephone apparatus, radio microphones and microbugs; plants, bulbs, trees, fruit, potatoes and other vegetables; live animals and birds and certain derivatives of rare species such as fur skins and plumage.

Further information from: HM Customs and Excise, Kent House, Upper Ground, London SE1 9PS (tel: 01-928 0533).

CURRENCY

The pound (£) consists of 100 pence. Coins are issued to the value of 1p, 2p, 5p, 10p, 20p, 50p, £1. Notes are £1 (Scotland only), £5, £10, £20 and £50. Separate coins are issued in the Channel Islands and Isle of Man: they can only be used in these regions. Scotland has separate banknotes usually accepted throughout England. Pre-decimal terms are still used in street markets – 'half-a-crown' is 12½p; 'fivers' and 'tenners' are £5 and £10 notes respectively.

Banks open 0930–1530 Mon. to Fri., some larger branches also open 1630–1800 Thurs. In Scotland banks close at lunchtime Mon.–Thurs. from 1230–1330, with late opening Thurs. 1630–1800. Most banks close Sat., Sun., and public holidays (see p. 25), some bank branches open on Saturdays in England and Scotland. The Trustee Savings Bank of Scotland also opens its Cameron Toll Branch, Edinburgh, on a Sunday. All provide facilities for the exchange of traveller's checks and foreign currency (take your passport). Banks offer the best rate of exchange; rates quoted at exchange bureaux and travel agents (both have the same opening hours as shops) are often less favourable. Hotels, restaurants and shops, when accepting traveller's checks, usually charge commission above that of the banks.

Credit cards issued by international organizations are valid in larger shops and good-class restaurants. But you should be sure to carry enough cash/traveller's checks when travelling beyond urban areas to cover the possibility of non-acceptance of credit cards locally.

INTERNAL TRAVEL

From Seaports and Airports You can travel from Britain's ports by rail to London and other principal cities; there are also coach or bus services (coach is the term for a long-distance bus). The ports' Tourist Information Centres will have full details. If arriving by air, there are rail, coach, taxi or air services to take you to your first night's destination. From London (Heathrow) Airport you can reach Central London in about 40 minutes by Underground or Airbus no. 1, 2 or 3; taking a taxi is much more expensive. From London (Gatwick) Airport, express trains leave for Central London (Victoria Station) every 15 minutes in the day and hourly at night; the journey takes about 30 minutes.

Domestic Flights A network of routes connects Britain's major cities, as well as linking the mainland with the Channel Islands, Isles of Scilly, Isle of Man, Western Isles of Scotland, Orkney and Shetland (pp.14–15).

Passengers on British Airways' 'Shuttle' services between London and Edinburgh, Glasgow and Manchester, need check in only 10 minutes before departure and a seat on the aircraft is guaranteed.

Domestic flight details from airline main offices or local travel agent.

British Airways, 1st floor, Technical Block C, Hatton Cross, Hounslow, Middx (tel: 01-897 4000).

British Caledonian Airways (tel: 01-668 4222 and Crawley (0293) 27890).

British Midland Airways (tel: Derby (0332) 810552).

Dan-Air (tel: 01-680 1011).

Air UK, incorporating British Island Airways, (tel: 01-249 7073 and Norwich (0603) 44244/44288).

Brymon Airways, serving West Country, (tel: Plymouth (0752) 707023).

Loganair, serving Scotland, (tel: 041-889 3181).

By Rail British Rail's Inter-City trains are fast, frequent and comfortable; local trains operating cross-country serving small towns and resorts are not quite so efficient. Most main-line trains have restaurant/buffet cars and there are comfortable sleeping cars on overnight journeys. There are two classes of travel, 1st class being about 50% more expensive than 2nd class, but many special discount fares are available, particularly at weekends and at off-peak periods. More information from travel agents, main stations, British Rail Travel Centre (see Useful Addresses p. 25). See p.17 for Motorail car-carrying service and Rail Drive provision of self-drive cars at stations.)

In London it is essential to go to the correct main station, all have an Underground station on or near the premises. Main London terminals (destinations in brackets): **Charing Cross** (Kent and East Sussex); **Euston** (Birmingham, Manchester, Liverpool, North Wales, North West England, Glasgow, Western Scotland); **King's Cross** (North-East England and Eastern Scotland – including York, Newcastle, Edinburgh, Aberdeen); **Liverpool Street** (East Anglia); **Paddington** (South West England, West Midlands, Cardiff and South Wales); **St Pancras** (Midlands and South Yorkshire – including Leicester, Nottingham, Derby, Sheffield); **Victoria** (Kent, Surrey, Sussex); **Waterloo** (Southern England – Surrey, Hampshire, Dorset, South Devon).

If you plan to do much travelling by rail, the BritRail Pass gives overseas visitors unlimited travel for periods of 8, 15, 22 days or one month (1st or 2nd class). The Youth Pass offers the same facilities (2nd class only) to young people aged 14–26. These Passes cannot be bought in Britain and must be obtained before you leave home from leading travel agents and overseas offices of British Rail. Rail Rover Passes, which allow unlimited travel in specified areas for a 7-day period, can be bought in Britain.

By Coach The most economical way of travelling is by coach (long-distance bus) although in general, journeys take much longer than by rail. A network of coach services covers Britain, enabling you to reach every major town – with local bus connections to neighbouring towns and villages. Advance booking is advisable for long-distance services departing from London. Tickets from Victoria Coach Station, Buckingham Palace Rd, London SW1 (tel: 01-730 0202).

Britexpress Travelcard gives adult overseas visitors a discount of one-third off the standard fare for any number of journeys taken during 30 consecutive days on all National Express Services in England, Wales, Scottish Citylink coaches, London-Scottish services and on certain other services of associated companies. Available at Victoria Coach Station (address above), London Heathrow and London Gatwick airports; East Kent Road Car, Pencester Road, Dover; Eastern Scottish, St Andrew's Bus Station, Edinburgh; Western Scottish, Buchanan Bus Station, Glasgow.

By Bus Local bus services offer flexibility of travel and are moderately priced. Details of fares and timetables from local bus stations and Tourist Information Centres. At many bus stops, panels on the post indicate the route served and frequency of service.

By Taxi Black 'London' Taxis have a yellow sign illuminated when they are available for hire. The fare is shown on the meter along with a notice of supplementary charges. The usual tip is 10–15% of the fare. Radio-linked taxis and mini-cabs cannot be hailed in the street but must be ordered by telephone. Hotels have the numbers and they are also found in the Yellow Pages telephone directory. If you are hiring a cab for a long journey it's advisable to ask the approximate fare before departure.

Organized Excursions Day and half-day guided tours are available to places throughout Britain. In London, check with London Transport and National Travel (see Useful Addresses p. 25); Tourist Information Centres will also have local details.

OFFSHORE ISLANDS

Shetland

By boat P&O overnight car ferry departs Aberdeen 1800 hours Mon., Wed., Fri. all year, arriving Lerwick approx. 0800. P&O also run long weekend mini-cruises April, May, June, Sept. Contact: P&O Ferries, P.O. Box 5, Jamiesons Quay, Aberdeen (tel: Aberdeen (0224) 572615). **By air** four British Airways flights daily, Aberdeen to Sumburgh. Also flights most days from Inverness, Edinburgh and Glasgow.

Orkney

By boat from Scrabster to Stromness by P&O car ferry, up to five times a day June–Sept., daily, except Sun., Oct.–May. Contact: P&O Ferries Terminal, Pierhead, Stromness (tel: Stromness (0856) 850655). Passenger ferries from John o'Groats to South Ronaldsay, May–Sept. Contact: Thomas & Bews, Windiekap, Brough, Caithness (tel: Barrock (084 785) 619 or John o'Groats (095 581) 353). **By air** two British Airways flights Mon.–Fri. from Aberdeen to Kirkwall, connecting with planes from Heathrow. Flights from other Scottish airports by British Airways and Loganair (tel: Kirkwall (0856) 3457).

Outer Hebrides

By boat Caledonian MacBrayne run a car-ferry service to every island except Benbecula (no commercial port). Ferry to Lewis leaves from Ullapool; ferries to Harris and North Uist depart from Uig on Skye; ferries to South Uist and Barra leave from Oban. At least one boat runs daily to each island, except Barra, which has four weekly, June–end Sept., and three in winter. Contact: Caledonian MacBrayne Ltd, Ferry Terminal, Gourock (tel: Gourock (0475) 33755). **By air** daily flight (except Sun.) by British Airways to Stornoway via Inverness or Glasgow. British Airways also fly daily Glasgow to Benbecula. Loganair flies to Barra from Glasgow daily (except Sun.).

Inner Hebrides

For those wishing to visit several islands, 8- or 12-day Highlands and Islands Travelpass gives unlimited travel on most buses, trains, ferries. (If purchased overseas, it is valid for 5 or 10 days). Contact: Travelpass, Hi-Line, Holiday Lodge, Bridgend Road, Dingwall, Ross-shire, Scotland. An invaluable guide, *Getting Around the Highlands and Islands*, is available to callers at Scottish Tourist Information Centres or from Highlands and Islands Development Board, 27 Bank St., Inverness.

Islay: By boat Ferry service from Kennacraig, Kintyre, 6km/4mi S of Tarbert. Caledonian MacBrayne sail to Port Ellen, or Port Askaig twice daily; May–Sept. Timetables and reservations: Caledonian MacBrayne Ltd, Ferry Terminal, Gourock (tel: Gourock (0475) 33950). **By air** Loganair service Glasgow to Islay, two flights a day Mon.–Fri. and one on Sat. (tel: 041-889 3181).

Jura: By boat Western Ferries car ferry sails from Port Askaig on Islay to Feolin about 12 times a day weekdays, Sun. four times, May–Sept. During winter, 11 times a day Mon.–Fri., seven a day Sat., two on Sun. Timetables and reservations: Western Ferries, 16 Woodside Crescent, Glasgow (tel: 041-332 9766).

Mull: By boat Caledonian MacBrayne's car-ferry service runs from Oban to Craignure five times a day weekdays, Sun. four times, May–Sept.; restricted winter service. (See Islay for address.)

Iona A bus from Craignure on Mull goes to the Iona ferry at Fionnphort three times daily, once on Sun. The Iona passenger ferry runs frequently every day in summer, but not Sun. in winter. Caledonian McBrayne runs a Sacred Isle Cruise from Oban twice a week on Tues., and Thurs., (see Islay for address).

Skye: By boat ferry from Kyle of Lochalsh to Kyleakin takes 5 mins; from Mallaig to Armadale 30 mins. Restricted winter services (passengers only in winter). Contact: Caledonian MacBrayne (tel: Gourock (0475) 33755). **By air** Loganair flies from Glasgow to Broadford once a day weekdays June–Sept., restricted winter service (tel: 041-889 3181).

Arran

By boat car ferry from Ardrossan to Brodick (one hour) five sailings daily; or Claonaig (Kintyre) to Lochranza (30 mins) eight sailings daily, May–Sept. only. Contact: Caledonian MacBrayne Ltd, Ferry Terminal, Gourock (tel: Gourock (0475) 34568).

Caledonian MacBrayne also offer services to other Scottish offshore islands – tel: Gourock (0475) 34568 for more information.

Isle of Man

By boat Steam Packet Co. car ferries sail daily all year, Douglas to Heysham. In summer, Steam Packet Co. sails between Douglas and Fleetwood, Ardrossan, Belfast, Dublin. Contact: The Steam Packet Co., P.O. Box 5, Douglas, Isle of Man (tel: Douglas (0624) 23344). **By air** flights daily to Ronaldsway Airport from main airports like Liverpool, Manchester, London (Heathrow); less frequent services from other airports.

Isle of Wight

Passengers Sealink ferry links Portsmouth–Ryde. Rail connections with Brading, Sandown, Shanklin. Hovercraft from Portsmouth to Ryde is fastest (7 mins); Hovertravel (tel: Portsmouth (0705) 829988 or Ryde (0983) 65241; Hydrofoil, Southampton–Cowes: Red Funnel Services (tel: Southampton (0703) 226211 or (0703) 33042 after office hours; or Cowes (0983) 292704). **Cars** Sealink Ferry, Portsmouth–Fishbourne and Lymington–Yarmouth (tel: Portsmouth (0705) 827744); local Red Funnel Line, Southampton–Cowes (tel: Southampton (0703) 226211).

Isles of Scilly

By boat March–Oct. Penzance–St Mary's, departs Mon.–Fri., 0930; Sat. 0930 until May then 0630 and 1345 hours. Contact: Isles of Scilly Steamship Co. Ltd, St Mary's, Isles of Scilly (tel: Scillonia (0720) 22357). **By air** seven flights most days until end Oct. by helicopter from Penzance to St Mary's. Restricted winter services. Contact: British Airways

Helicopters, Penzance Heliport (tel: Penzance (0736) 3871/2). Brymon Airways fly to St Mary's from Newquay, Plymouth and Exeter with connecting services from Heathrow and Gatwick. Contact: Brymon Airways, City Airport, Roborough, Plymouth (tel: Plymouth (0752) 705151).

The Channel Islands

By boat Sealink operate passenger/car ferries from Weymouth and Portsmouth to Guernsey and Jersey. Daily crossings in summer; six days a week in winter. From Portsmouth – overnight journey in luxury cabins; day journey from Weymouth. Advance booking is essential. Sealink also offer special packages (tel: Portsmouth (0705) 755111; Weymouth (0305) 786363). Channel Island Ferries operates a Portsmouth–Jersey–Guernsey service leaving Portsmouth at 1000 daily in summer; six days a week in winter. For reservations tel: Portsmouth (0705) 819416.

By air flights from airports throughout Britain to Jersey and Guernsey. Aurigny Air Services Ltd offer seven flights to Alderney daily from Southampton and Bournemouth. (tel: Eastleigh (0703) 612829).

IF YOU ARE MOTORING

If overseas visitors, bringing their own cars to Britain, are members of a motoring organization in their own country, which is affiliated to the Fédération Internationale de l'Automobile (FIA) or the Commonwealth Motoring Conference (CMC), then they can make use of the reciprocal facilities provided by the two British clubs: Automobile Association (AA), Fanum House, Basingstoke, Hants (tel: Basingstoke (0256) 20123; Royal Automobile Club, RAC House, PO Box 100, Landsdowne Road, Croydon (tel: 01-686 2525). (In Scotland; Royal Scottish Automobile Club, 11 Blythswood Square, Glasgow G2 4AG.) Both clubs maintain offices at all ports of entry for car-carrying ferries.

Documents Visitors can drive in Britain on a current International Driving Permit or on their current domestic licence (which should be carried), up to a maximum of one year from their last date of entry to Britain. After this, a British driving licence must be obtained. Minimum age for driving a car or motorcycle with an engine larger than 50 c.c. is 17, for mopeds, 16. Also bring your car registration papers and a nationality plate/sticker.

Third-party insurance is compulsory, and you must bring an International Motor Insurance Card (Green Card), except for EEC citizens who should carry evidence of their existing insurance policy.

Petrol (gasoline) is sold both Imperial and Metric (1 gallon = 4.5 litres) and is graded by a star system ranging from low-quality two-star (minimum 90 octanes) to high-compression four-star (minimum 97 octanes). Most cars run well on three- or four-star (94, 97 octanes). If you are travelling into remote country areas, particularly in Scotland, it's advisable to carry a spare can of fuel as garages or filling stations are scarce. Very few garages throughout Britain operate a 24-hour service, so stock up before 1800 hours.

Rules of the Road

The following information is a brief résumé of Britain's motoring laws and is intended only as a guide. For official information, consult *The Highway Code*, obtainable at British bookshops.

Roads Generally major roads are well maintained and there are no tolls except at a limited number of bridges and tunnels. Drive on the left and overtake on the right. Give way to vehicles approaching from the right at traffic islands. Roads are classified M (motorway), A (main roads), B (minor roads).

Speed Maximum speed in built-up areas with street lamp-posts is 30 miles per hour (48kph). Outside built-up areas and on motorways, speed limits vary according to speed signs; usual maximum is 70 miles per hour (112kph) on motorways, and 60 miles per hour (96kph) on single lane roads.

Road markings White lines: solid single or double line across road means stop; triangle and broken double line mean yield right-of-way; broken lines along the road indicate traffic lane and centre line; double line in centre of road prohibits crossing; double line with one line broken indicates no crossing if the nearer line is unbroken – crossing permitted when road is clear if broken line is nearer. Yellow lines at roadside: single, no waiting during working day; double, no waiting during working day and additional times. Check the times of no waiting, shown on nearby signs.

Signs Warning signs are triangles with a red border, with the nature of the warning in black. Signs giving orders are circular with a red border, with the nature of the order in black. Information signs are mostly rectangular with a blue background. Direction signs are mostly rectangular: blue on or near motorways, green or white on other roads.

Lights must be used in the period half an hour after sunset to half an hour before sunrise; also in conditions of poor visibility during the day.

Horns must not be used on a restricted road between 2330–0700 or at any time when the vehicle is stationary.

Safety belts and helmets The wearing of seat belts by drivers and front seat passengers is compulsory. Also it is compulsory for motorcycle and moped riders (and pillion passengers) to wear safety helmets. Carry a red **warning sign** (a reflecting triangle) in case of breakdown.

Breakdowns Get your vehicle off the road if possible and keep passengers off the road. Telephone the nearest service garage. The telephone operator (dial 100) will give you the number. It's advisable to carry with you items which might not be available in small local garages, *eg* distributor cap, set of points, radiator hose, fan belt and fuses. You may be able to rent breakdown kits from motoring organizations in your own country.

Accidents It is a driver's duty to stop and report an accident involving any other vehicle, persons, most domesticated animals, or roadside property, to anyone who has reasonable grounds to request name, address and details of insurance policy, or to a police station within 24 hours. The driver of any vehicle involved in an accident should note the registration number of any other vehicle involved, take names and addresses of witnesses, and make a sketch of the area where the accident has occurred.

If injury has occurred, dial 999 from the nearest telephone and ask for police and ambulance. If there is no call-box or house with a phone near the scene of the accident, ask any motorist to drive to the nearest place to make the call. Do not go too far from the accident yourself.

Driving offences Exceeding the speed limit, reckless or dangerous driving, causing death by dangerous driving and driving without due care and attention are among serious offences involving heavy fines and/or imprisonment. These offences usually also involve endorsement of licence or disqualification from driving.

Drink or drug offences A heavy fine and/or imprisonment may be imposed on a driver convicted of driving, attempting to drive, or being in charge of a vehicle (even if it is not in motion) while unfit through drink or drugs. A uniformed policeman can require a driver to submit to a breathalyzer test. If it indicates the presence of alcohol in excess of 80 milligrams in 100 millilitres of blood, the policeman may arrest the driver and arrange for a blood or urine test.

London 6 weeks in advance
Reservations for Rooms in advance

Tyres It is an offence to drive with tyres which are not properly inflated or have a severe cut. The tread pattern must have a depth of *at least* 1mm throughout three-quarters of the breadth and around the entire outer circumference. You should also ensure that all parts of your vehicle such as indicators, brakes, mirror, *etc*, are in good working order.

Parking Roadside parking is permitted provided signs do not indicate otherwise. Much city-centre roadside parking is only permitted at meters, usually for a maximum of two hours. Off-street parking in underground and multistory car parks is indicated by signs with a white P on a blue background. Most car parks make a minimum charge for two hours. In some residential parts of towns, parking is restricted to local residents holding permits (check signs). Vehicles illegally parked are liable to be ticketed, or in London, wheel-clamped and may be towed away by the police to compounds. (Apply at nearest police station.)

Motorail

British Rail operates a Motorail service to take you and your car in the same train to different parts of Britain. But space is limited and you should book in advance. Details from principal stations and British Rail Travel Centre (see Useful Addresses p. 25).

Car Rental

There are car rental facilities at most of Britain's points of entry; otherwise consult the telephone directory. Hertz, Avis and Godfrey Davis are leading companies; the last two offer a Rail Drive service which includes the provision of self-drive cars to await your arrival at main-line railway stations. Rent-it-here, leave-it-there services are available where there are local depots. Rental conditions vary, but in most cases visitors must have held a full driving licence for 12 months. There's usually a statutory charge payable in advance, plus an additional deposit for insurance, and a further charge based on length of rental or mileage. A discount is normally given for four weeks and rates are often much less in winter.

Avis Rent A Car, Trident House, Station Rd, Hayes, Middlesex (tel: car rental: 01-848 8733; chauffeur-driven: 01-897 2621).

Godfrey Davis Ltd, Bushey House, High Street, Bushey, Watford (tel: Car hire Central reservations 01-950 5050; chauffeur-driven 01-834 6701).

Hertz Rent A Car Head Office, 1272 London Rd, London SW6 (tel: 01-679 1799).

WHERE TO STAY

Britain offers a variety of accommodation at all price levels, so you can take your pick from large modern hotels, motels, small family hotels, historic house hotels and medieval inns with up-to-date amenities – or you can stay at a guest house or on a farm. If you prefer to cater for yourself there are trailer (caravan) and campsites throughout Britain, as well as apartments, houses, cottages and chalets.

Booking It is a good plan to reserve accommodation before leaving your own country, especially during July/August, and all year round if you plan to stay in Central London. This can be done through your travel agent or one of the overseas representatives of British hotels or by writing or telephoning direct. The British Tourist Authority and Tourist Boards for England, Scotland and Wales publish comprehensive guides covering all aspects of accommodation including self-catering in all parts of Britain (see Useful Addresses p. 25). It's advisable to call in at your nearest British Tourist Authority for advice or to send for official Tourist Board guides before arrival in Britain so that you can plan ahead. Guides are also available at Tourist Information Centres throughout Britain and the Automobile Association publishes a wide range of guides available at British bookshops.

If you have not booked in advance, a variety of reservation services are available when you reach Britain. Many hotel groups have Central Reservation Offices through which you can reserve rooms in member hotels, and there are numerous booking agencies in London and other major cities. Several have offices at airports and main railway stations.

Wherever you go in Britain, Tourist Information Centres (TICs) will help you find accommodation for the night and nearly all of them can make provisional reservations for the same night in their own area (personal callers only). Many TICs also operate a Book-a-Bed-Ahead service (in Wales, the Bed Booking Service), by which they can reserve a night's accommodation in a different part of the country, provided that your destination is in an area where the service operates. There is usually a small booking fee and, in Scotland, you pay a deposit which is deducted from your hotel bill.

London It's advisable to book well in advance of arrival. Your own local office of the British Tourist Authority (see Useful Addresses p. 25) will advise, or write six weeks in advance to the London Visitor and Convention Bureau, 26 Grosvenor

Gardens, London SW1. Alternatively, book ahead through a travel agent or worldwide hotel group. It is not essential to stay in Central London as public transport from inner London boroughs is fast and easy. If you arrive without pre-booking, go immediately to the Tourist Information Centre at London (Heathrow) Airport, or at Victoria Railway Station and they will book a room for you. Members of the Youth Hostel Association can stay in London at Holland Park, Kensington; West Hill, Highgate, N6; 36 Carter Lane, EC4; Bolton Gardens, SW5.

Charges Breakfast is usually included in the quoted price for a night's hotel accommodation. For longer stays, many hotels offer an all-in price for 'full-board' (bed, breakfast, lunch, dinner) or 'half-board' (bed, breakfast and one main meal).

Charges for self-catering accommodation are usually on a weekly basis. All household requirements are supplied, but you may have to pay extra for gas, electricity, linen. The deposit on self-catering accommodation is payable before taking possession of the premises.

Reservations and Cancellations To ensure that you do not pay more than you intended, always ask for the total cost of your accommodation, inclusive of meals, service charge and Value Added Tax (VAT), before making your reservation. When booking in advance you may be asked to pay a deposit, especially when written confirmation is not possible.

If you have to cancel a reservation, do so as soon as possible, or the management may claim compensation, since a booking confirmed by both management and guest is regarded as a legal contract binding both parties.

Accommodation

Hotels and Motels Plenty of large modern hotels and motels with car-parking space are situated throughout Britain. Most rooms have a private bathroom, television, radio and telephone, and are centrally heated. Motels are usually found alongside main roads. In country areas many splendid mansions and even castles – once the private homes of nobility – are now comfortable hotels. Here you will probably be surrounded with antique furniture and may even sleep in a four-poster bed!

Country Inns Despite the addition of modern amenities, many old inns retain their historic atmosphere. The majority have 6–20 bedrooms and, as well as character, usually offer excellent meals.

Guest Houses Accommodation in these small private houses is clean and adequate. Most guest houses are unlicensed

and have no bar, but there is usually a comfortable lounge with television. You can choose either bed, breakfast and evening meal or just bed and breakfast.

Bed and Breakfast Many small private houses display a Bed & Breakfast sign. You don't need to book your room in advance – just call in and stay for a night or two. Accommodation is clean and comfortable and even cheaper than in a guest house. In most cases, only breakfast is provided.

Farmhouse Accommodation You don't need to book in advance for this simple, inexpensive type of accommodation – just look for roadside signs directing you to a farm with accommodation available. As with guest houses, some farms serve breakfast and evening meals, while others offer just bed and breakfast.

Tents and Trailers Your local British Tourist Authority office will have details of Britain's registered sites, both for tents and touring trailers, and for permanently-sited trailers. It is advisable to book sites in advance. You are not restricted to registered sites, but *remember that if you wish to camp on private land you must first obtain the consent of the landowner or his tenant.* It is not permitted to camp overnight on roadside verges.

The International Camping Carnet is not a requirement for using commercial campsites in Britain. If you are towing a trailer, it is necessary to ensure that your insurance cover includes towed vehicles. If you rent a trailer in Britain, the rental agency will arrange appropriate insurance. Trailers under tow are restricted to a speed limit of 50mph (80kph) and on three-lane motorways they may not enter the third (fast) lane. Cars with trailers may not use meter-controlled parking spaces.

Youth Hostels Hostel accommodation is cheap but spartan, usually in dormitories. Meals or cooking facilities are normally provided. It's best to book well ahead and many are open April–Oct. only.

Reservations are made with individual hostels and you pay in advance. You'll need an International YHA card which you can obtain in your home country, or buy an International Guest Membership card from the London office at 14 Southampton St., WC2 (tel: 01-836 8541).

Handbooks from headquarters: YHA (England and Wales), Trevelyan House, 8 St Stephen's Hill, St Albans, Herts. SYHA (Scotland), 7 Glebe Crescent, Stirling. The YMCA and YWCA also have hostels. Lists and bookings: National Council of YMCAs, 640 Forest Rd, Walthamstow, London E17 (tel: 01-520 5599) and YWCA Headquarters, 2 Weymouth St., London W1 (tel: 01-631 0657).

FOOD & DRINK

British cooking is generally simple, straightforward and – at its best – delicious. What nicer way of starting the day than with a traditional breakfast of bacon and eggs? Roast beef and Yorkshire pudding (baked batter) and roast lamb with mint sauce are rightly renowned as national dishes . . . then there's Britain's splendid array of cheeses – Stilton, Caerphilly, Cheddar – to name just a few. Afternoon Tea is a particularly British treat with muffins, crumpets and rich fruit cakes like Dundee Cake to enjoy, or – in the West Country – Cream Teas with scones, jam and cream. In Northern England and Scotland, High Tea is so substantial that it's like an early excuse for supper!

Many parts of Britain have their own specialities – mentioned in the introductions to the regions in the gazetteer. Restaurants serving regional dishes are now much easier to locate, thanks to the Taste of England scheme, sponsored by the English Tourist Board, which encourages hotels and restaurants to serve traditional English food, using fresh local produce wherever possible. Regional tourist boards in England and Tourist Information Centres can also advise on local specialities. Scotland and Wales both have their own variations of the scheme and their respective Tourist Boards produce lists of participants.

All reputable restaurants and cafés now display a menu outside. Quoted prices should be assessed against any extras mentioned in small print. Meals are subject to the addition of Value Added Tax (VAT is a variable tax shown separately on a bill for services, but included in the purchase price of goods) and there may also be cover and service charges. Where there is no service charge, the normal tip for satisfactory service is 10–15%.

For those on a budget, Britain offers a wide selection of inexpensive eating-places. Café chains like Wimpy Bars, Happy Eater and Little Chef concentrate on grills and hamburgers; then there are the English branches of American pizza houses and hamburger cafés like McDonalds. Most towns have French and Italian inspired bistros which offer an interesting ambience and competitive prices, while wine bars usually have salads, pâtés and cheese on offer.

Steak-house chains, including Berni Inns and Schooner Inns, tend to produce the same standard of quality and service in each establishment with prices on the high side of moderate. Large city-centre department stores often have moderately priced restaurants within their premises, catering particularly for shoppers – with or without children. Good places for family groups are hotels, many of which welcome nonresidents for meals, while throughout Britain you can find restaurants specializing in the cuisine of various countries – French, Italian, Greek, Chinese, Indian, Polish, *etc.*

Most restaurants (not cafés) are licensed to provide alcoholic drinks with meals; they will also supply water if asked (all British tap water is drinkable). Residents staying in hotels may order alcoholic drinks with or without food at any time of day. Soft drinks include the usual coca-cola, fizzy orange and lemon. Be sure to ask for *fresh* orange or lemon if you want natural juice. Tea is the universal hot drink, followed closely by coffee – which may be instant coffee in cheaper cafés.

For local atmosphere and a quick inexpensive lunch, try a pub (public house). Some pubs have a separate restaurant with waiter service; most have counter service whereby dishes can be ordered at the bar and eaten there – soup, salads, shepherd's pie, bangers and mash (sausage and mashed potato). Sandwiches are usually available, also 'ploughmans' – bread, cheese, pickle. It is customary to buy a drink with snacks and although tipping is not expected, bartenders always appreciate the offer of a drink.

Under current licensing laws, English pubs generally open 1100–1500 and 1730–2300, with shorter hours on Sunday. Hours vary slightly from place to place and, at time of going to press, the licensing hours may soon be reviewed. In London opening hours tend to be longer than elsewhere, although bars in Scotland are open all day in some town and city centres. Licensing laws differ slightly in Wales and on Sundays in some parts you may not be able to drink except as a hotel resident. People under 18 years are not permitted in British pubs.

Beer is ordered in pints and half-pints (one imperial pint = 20 fluid oz.) and the main types are bitter (ask for 'draught'), pale ale, brown ale (bottled), stout and lager. Beer is not served chilled and many regions have their own special brew – mentioned later in the gazetteer. Recent years have seen a growth in the consumer movement, the Campaign for Real Ale (CAMRA), which publishes *The Good Beer Guide* and fights for the retention of old-style beer without the artificial addition of carbon dioxide gas.

Take-away alcoholic drinks are sold in wine and spirit shops (called 'off licences'), some pubs, department stores and supermarkets. European and American beers are usually available in cans, often brewed under licence in Britain rather than imported. The standard content of a British bottle of spirits (gin, vodka, Scotch, brandy) is 75 centilitres, but since Britain joined the EEC, many bottles of spirits and wine hold a litre (100 centilitres).

Shops selling take-away food – often Chinese and Indian – are found in most towns as are Britain's famous fish and chip shops, although these are rapidly being replaced by take-away pizza and hamburger bars. Generally, the right time to get hungry is – for breakfast: 0730–0930; lunch: 1200–1400; tea: 1500–1700; dinner: 1900–2100.

ENJOY YOURSELF

An International Reply Coupon should be enclosed with any enquiry to addresses given in this section.

Cricket Hampshire gave birth to the game as it is known today, but almost every English town and village fields a cricket team during the season (May–Sept.). Important matches take place between counties, with internationals (Test matches) against other countries, notably Australia and the West Indies. London has both Lord's in St John's Wood, NW8, and the Oval, Kennington, SE11; other important grounds include Headingley near Leeds and Old Trafford, Manchester. Contact: Marylebone Cricket Club, Lord's Cricket Ground, London NW8.

Fishing Britain's lakes, rivers, ponds are all owned by a person or organization and you must have permission to fish in them; a fee is usually payable. In Scotland you only need the owner's permission, but in England and Wales ten regional water authorities control freshwater fishing and a licence is always needed for salmon and trout fishing and usually for coarse fishing. Sea-fishing doesn't require a licence, except for sea-trout from estuaries. Licences are obtainable from water authorities, fishing-tackle shops, hotels and clubs in the area.

In England and Wales there are regulations about the size of fish you can catch and any fish smaller than the limit must be put back; Scotland imposes no limitations. A minimum close season, when fishing is banned, allows for breeding. This is organized by local water authorities and the close season varies between regions, although it generally operates from end Oct. until April or May. A statutory close season for coarse fishing (15 March–16 June) and for game fishing (salmon: 1 Nov.–31 Jan.; trout, excluding rainbow trout: 1 Oct.–24 March) is enforced in England and Wales, although not in Scotland. Contact: The National Federation of Anglers, Halliday House, 2, Wilson Street, Derby. For local water authorities, consult the telephone directory or dial 192 for Directory Enquiries.

Football For details of soccer and rugby matches, see local newspapers or ask at a library or Tourist Information Centre.

Golf Britain has many 9-hole and 18-hole courses, particularly at seaside resorts; some courses belong to hotels while others are owned by the local authority. Information from: English Golf Union, 12A Denmark St., Wokingham, Berkshire; Royal and Ancient Golf Club, St Andrews, Fife, Scotland.

Hunting and Shooting For information on hunting, contact: British Field Sports Society, 59 Kennington Rd, London SE1. For shooting, contact: National Rifle Association, Bisley Camp, Brookwood, Woking, Surrey; Clay Pigeon Shooting Association, 107 Epping New Rd, Buckhurst Hill, Essex.

Organized Holidays The Sports Council organizes residential holidays at places throughout Britain, with expert tuition in the sport of your choice, including archery, golf, sailing, badminton, tennis, water skiing. Information from: Sports Council, Dept. B, 70 Brompton Rd, London SW3.

The following organizations run courses on various subjects throughout Britain:

Field Studies Council, Preston Montford, Montford Bridge, Shrewsbury, Shropshire (ecology, birds, geography, conservation).

Association for Cultural Exchange, Babraham, Cambridge, Cambs. (architecture, theatre, writers).

Embassy Hotels Ltd, Station St., Burton upon Trent, Staffs. (weekend courses – canals, pottery, photography, wine, antiques, heritage).

Galleon World Travel Association Ltd, Galleon House, King St., Maidstone, Kent (natural history, music, archaeology).

Pony Trekking, Riding, Showjumping, Horse Racing Ponies of Britain is the national pony-trekking body. For information about approved centres, including details of social activities, accommodation and what to wear, write to: Ponies of Britain, Brookside Farm, Ascot, Berkshire.

The British Horse Society, the official riding organization, issues a list of approved riding schools, indicating standards of instruction reached and accommodation available. Contact: British Horse Society, British Equestrian Centre, Stoneleigh, Kenilworth, Warwickshire.

The headquarters of the British Show-jumping Association is also at Equestrian Centre (address above). Highlights of the Showjumping year are the Royal International Horse Show (June) and Horse of the Year Show (Oct.), both at Wembley, London. Other events include All England shows at Hickstead, West Sussex (Easter, May, July, Aug.); Royal Windsor Horse Show (May); Greater London Horse Show on Clapham Common (summer Bank holiday); Olympia International Show, London (Dec.).

Horse trials are held at Badminton in Gloucestershire; Tidworth, Hampshire; Bramham Park, North Yorkshire; Burghley, Lincolnshire; and there's a race meeting virtually every weekday somewhere in Britain. For information on Flat and National Hunt Racing, contact: Racing Information Bureau, Winkfield Road, Ascot, Berkshire.

Soccer (see Football)

Tennis Most towns have public courts which can be reserved for a small fee – ask at a local library or Tourist Information Centre. Many courts are private and you will need to enquire at the club-house whether temporary membership can be arranged. The highlight of the tennis year, the **Lawn Tennis Championships** are held at Wimbledon, London SW19, during June's last week and the first week of July.

Walking, Climbing and Mountaineering Britain has countless miles of footpaths and bridleways, some of which take the walker into parts reached by no other means. Ordnance Survey maps (1:50,000/1¼in:1 mile) cover much of the area. The Ramblers' Association 1–5 Wandsworth Rd, London SW8, is the principal body for organized rambling and hill walking; write for advice on all aspects and membership details.

Britain also has several long-distance footpaths, controlled by the Countryside Commission: Pennine Way (400km/250mi, Edale in Derbyshire to Kirk Yetholm in Scotland); Cleveland Way (150km/93mi, Yorkshire moors to coast); Pembrokeshire Coast Path in south-west Wales (267km/167mi); Offa's Dyke (269km/168mi through the Welsh Marches); South Downs Way in Sussex (128km/80mi); North Downs Way across Surrey and Kent (223km/140mi); Ridgeway Path (136km/85mi, Overton Hill to Ivinghoe Beacon in Buckinghamshire); South-West Peninsula Coast Path

(824km/515mi, Minehead to Poole in Dorset). Contact: Countryside Commission (National Parks and Long-Distance Footpaths), John Dower House, Crescent Place, Cheltenham, Gloucestershire.

Scotland's first long-distance footpath, West Highland Way (150km/95mi, from north of Glasgow to Fort William) was opened in 1980, while the Southern Upland Way (328km/204mi, from Portpatrick to Cockburnspath through the Lammermuir Hills) is a more recent addition to the growing list of long-distance footpaths. Contact: Countryside Commission for Scotland, Battleby, Redgorton, Perth.

Careful preparation is essential before tackling any long-distance walking. You will need to have good boots, warm waterproof clothing, a compass, emergency food, maps and a whistle.

The Forestry Commission, (Forest Parks), 231 Corstorphine Rd, Edinburgh, will provide details of the information centres, nature trails and signposted walks through their Forest Parks. Similarly: The Nature Conservancy Council (Nature Reserves, Nature Parks and Nature Trails), Northminster House, Peterborough.

The British Mountaineering Council, the national body representing climbers, offers advice on all aspects of mountaineering. Information from: British Mountaineering Council, Crawford House, Precinct Centre, Booth St. East, Manchester.

Watersports The Royal Yachting Association (RYA) is Britain's national authority for sailing, power boating, motor cruising and boardsailing (windsurfing). It runs a National Proficiency and Coaching Scheme. A list of the RYA's recognized teaching places is obtainable from: Royal Yachting Association, Victoria Way, Woking, Surrey.

Many local clubs are affiliated to the RYA and offer such facilities as moorings, club-houses, launching slips, as well as instruction for beginners. If you're sailing round the coast, it's not necessary to join a club, although inland it is, since sailing rights on inland waters are often restricted to club membership. Sailing needn't be expensive as boats (and sometimes gear) can be rented from some centres.

The British Canoe Union publishes a list of clubs and publications. Write to: British Canoe Union, Flexel House, 45–47 High St., Addlestone, Weybridge, Surrey. Beginners can learn by taking a Sports Council course (see Organized Holidays p. 20) or by joining a club belonging to the BCU.

Since there is no general right of public

access to any non-tidal waters, a licence is needed to canoe on canals controlled by the British Waterways Board (about half Britain's inland waterway system). There is part-access to the Rivers Thames, Severn and Wye, but first check with water's owner where you can go. Contact: British Waterways Board, Pleasure Craft Licensing Officer, Willow Grange, Church Rd, Watford, Hertfordshire.

Many firms rent out self-drive motor cruisers for touring waterways. These accommodate 2–12 people, and charges vary according to season (noticeably lower in spring and autumn). Instruction on handling craft is given when you rent. Contact: British Waterways Board, Melbury House, Melbury Terrace, London NW1; British Waterways Board, Pleasure Craft Licensing Officer, (address above); Inland Waterways Association, 114 Regents Park Rd, London NW1; Association of Pleasure Craft Operators, Norbury Junction, Stafford.

Information about surfing, underwater swimming and water skiing is available respectively from: British Surfing Association, Room G 5, Burrow Chambers, East Burrow Road, Swansea, West Glamorgan; British Sub-Aqua Club, 16 Upper Woburn Place, London WC1; British Water Ski Federation, 390 City Road, London EC1.

ENTERTAINMENT

All kinds of traditional events take place throughout Britain all year round, so be sure to look for details in local newspapers and check with Tourist Information Centres. See also Festivals and Events under the regions of the gazetteer.

Festivals Many towns hold their own springtime festivals, such as Helston's Furry Dance and Padstow's 'Obby 'Oss (hobby-horse) festival in Cornwall, and the Flower Parade at Spalding, Lincolnshire. At Eastertime, you may see England's traditional morris men dancing to music in their colourful costumes. From May to August the old custom of well-dressing takes place in the Peak District, while traditional Highland Games are held in Scotland in July and August.

From spring to autumn there are music and drama festivals throughout Britain, eg Edinburgh's springtime Folk Festival and the music and dance of the summer International Musical Eisteddfod in Wales. Perhaps the finest is the Edinburgh International Festival, held in August, when the entire city takes on a lively, cosmopolitan air. But if you want to visit a real old English fair, then autumn is

the best time. The fairs at Widecombe and Barnstaple date back many years, as does Nottingham's famous Goose Fair, held at the beginning of October. In Scotland, the Arbroath Abbey Pageant in September commemorates the signing of Scottish Independence in 1320. In spring and autumn, many Welsh markets, such as those at Pwllheli, Bala and Dolgellau, expand into fairs. Autumn is also the time for Illuminations, with the bright lights of Morecambe and Blackpool providing a dazzling free spectacle.

London, of course, offers year-round pageantry such as the Changing of the Guard (daily in summer; alternate days in winter), but there are colourful annual events such as the Lord Mayor's Show in November. London is also the mecca for theatre-goers and concert-lovers.

Theatre Most London theatres maintain a tradition for their own kind of production: musicals at Her Majesty's, Palace and Drury Lane Theatre Royal (London's oldest); comedies and straight plays at Wyndham's, Queens, Phoenix, Globe, Lyric, Apollo, Criterion, and Theatre Royal, Haymarket; variety at the London Palladium and Prince of Wales. Classical drama, English and foreign, is performed at the National Theatre (which incorporates the Olivier, Lyttelton and Cottesloe theatres) and also by the Royal Shakespeare Company at the Barbican and The Pit. Classics are also produced at the Young Vic; (the Old Vic re-opened in 1983). Avant-garde productions can be seen at the Royal Court and at Riverside Studios, an arts centre in Hammersmith. Pubs, clubs and cellars comprise the venues for many fringe shows (see p. 30).

Most theatres have a matinée twice a week, usually Wed. and Sat.; evening performances (not Suns) start at 1930 or 2000. Tickets need not necessarily be expensive (fringe is usually cheaper than West End) and can be bought direct from box offices, through theatrical ticket agencies for a small charge, or through booking facilities found in larger hotels and stores. A kiosk in Leicester Square offers half-price theatre tickets for the same day only (Mon.–Sat. 1200–1400; 1430–1830).

Many provincial cities have excellent repertory theatres and standards are high, for example, at Bristol Old Vic, Liverpool Playhouse, Manchester's Royal Exchange, Birmingham Repertory, Glasgow Citizens and in university towns such as Oxford and Cambridge.

Opera and Ballet Britain has four major opera companies. Tickets cost about the same as for theatre, but you'll need to book well in advance.

The English National Opera performs in English at London Coliseum, St Martin's Lane, London WC2, and its subsidiary company, Opera North, is based in Leeds. There's also Welsh National Opera, based in Cardiff, and Scottish National Opera in Glasgow. Two venues outside London are also noted for opera – Glyndebourne in East Sussex, which offers a sumptuous setting, but is both very formal and expensive, and the Aldeburgh Festival in Suffolk.

The Royal Opera shares its home at London's Royal Opera House, Covent Garden, with the Royal Ballet. A smaller touring branch of the Royal Ballet called Sadler's Wells Royal Ballet, works from Sadler's Wells, Rosebery Ave, EC1. Two other touring companies, Ballet Rambert (contemporary dance), and London Festival Ballet, which stages new productions of classical or long-established works, and companies like the London Contemporary Dance Theatre and Scottish Ballet (based in Glasgow) bring dance in its myriad forms to Britain as a whole.

Concerts Most major cities in Britain have at least one symphony orchestra, and London has five. The principal concert venues in London are the Royal Festival Hall complex with its restaurant and bars, and the Barbican Hall in the Barbican Arts Centre (home of the London Symphony Orchestra and the English Chamber Orchestra), while the world-famous summer series of Henry Wood Promenade Concerts is held at the Royal Albert Hall. Outside London, a vast, varied number of works are performed virtually daily in all towns and cities, in halls, churches, cathedrals and universities throughout Britain. Check the review sections of Sunday newspapers – *The Observer, Sunday Times, Sunday Telegraph*, or ask at a Tourist Information Centre for details.

Cinemas Be prepared to queue for cinema seats unless you book in advance. Programmes run all week, starting around 1330 (1530 on Suns). The type of film is denoted by a censor's rating – U, PG, 15, 18. A U certificate indicates it is fit for all ages; PG (Parental Guidance) means that some scenes may be unsuitable for children; 15 means that children under 15 are not admitted; 18 admits no one under 18 years. Most large towns have cinemas showing popular, rather than specialist films, except in larger cities like Manchester and Edinburgh, which show both kinds. In London, arts films are shown at the National Film Theatre in the South Bank complex and the Institute of Contemporary Arts (ICA) in The Mall.

Television and Radio British television operates four channels. The British Broadcasting Corporation runs BBC 1 and BBC 2, neither of which carries advertising, while Independent Television offers two commercial channels – ITV and Channel 4. The BBC has four radio stations – 1 and 2 (light entertainment and pop music), 3 (classical music and drama), 4 (general entertainment and news). Many areas have their own local radio stations – London has two commercial stations. Television and radio programmes are published in daily newspapers and in the *Radio Times* (BBC) and *TV Times* (ITV).

WHAT YOU NEED TO KNOW

Chemists (pharmacies) with dispensing section for medicines open 0900–1730, usually with one late night opening – indicated on door. Every town/district has at least one dispensing chemist open Sundays and public holidays for one hour.

Churches Service times indicated in vestry; see also local newspapers and public library notice-boards.

Cigarettes Available from pubs, newsagents, supermarkets, grocers, vending-machines, railway stations. Popular foreign brands are generally available; more unusual brands are hard to find outside specialized tobacconists.

Closing times Shops generally open Mon.–Sat. 0900–1730. Most shops and restaurants closed Suns. Shops close at 1300 hours one weekday afternoon (usually Wed. or Thurs.). Central London stores have one late-night opening (Wed. or Thurs.). Many small shops and museums close for lunch (usually 1300–1400, but this varies). 'Last admission' to museums may be 30–45 minutes before advertised closing time.

Electricity Standard mains supply is 240 volts AC, 50 cycles. Overseas visitors may need converters/adaptors (bring with you). Many hotels supply adaptors for electric razors on request.

Health (See also p. 11). Unless you belong to an EEC country, or one with which the UK has a reciprocal health arrangement, visitors are now charged for the full cost of medical treatment in Britain – except in the case of accidents or emergencies requiring out-patient treatment only. It is therefore wise to take out medical insurance before leaving home. Residents of all EEC countries and Austria, Norway and Sweden can be treated under NHS arrangements provided that they have first obtained Form EIII to certify that they are entitled to medical benefits in their own country. Doctor's address: consult telephone directory or ask at post office.

Emergency: virtually every general hospital has a casualty department. For real emergencies, phone 999; you won't be charged for an ambulance if you need it. Dental treatment: similar services are available for dental emergencies – consult telephone directory under 'Dental Surgeons'. Further information on health regulations is available from British Tourist Authority offices.

Rabies It cannot be too strongly stressed that Britain totally prohibits the importation of live (or dead) animals from the rest of the world except under licence. One of the conditions of the licence is that animals are kept in approved quarantine premises for as long as six months in most cases (including domestic pets). No exemptions are allowed in respect of animals which have been vaccinated against rabies. Penalties for smuggling any creature involve imprisonment, unlimited fines and, in certain circumstances, destruction of the animal.

For details of animal importation and quarantine regulations apply to Ministry of Agriculture (Animal Health Division), Hook Rise South, Tolworth, Surbiton, Surrey KT6 7NF.

Lost property On British Rail trains and stations: lost property office at main-line terminal of rail region concerned. On Green Line Coaches: nearest Country Bus Services garage. On London Transport buses and Underground: 200 Baker Street, NW1. In street, park or elsewhere: call at a police station.

Newspapers The *International Herald Tribune*, a compilation of the *New York Times* and the *Washington Post*, is available from main city-centre newsagents and major railway stations, which often have European newspapers and magazines too.

Photography American, European and British colour films are sold at photography shops and chemists; processing takes about three days (longer in July/Aug.). Many museums and theatres forbid or restrict photography; it's best to check on entry.

Postal services Most post offices open 0900–1730 Mon.–Fri. and 0900–1230 Sat. Street post boxes are red. Postage stamps are only sold at post offices or, in country areas, at the sub-post office section of a shop. Check with postal clerks for all airmail and inland rates. Surface mail is not much cheaper than airmail for letters/cards. Overseas parcel rates vary according to destination. A customs declaration, from post offices, must be completed.

If you have no fixed address in Britain, you can receive mail through the Post Office's Poste Restante service. You pay a nominal fee for each letter received. For-

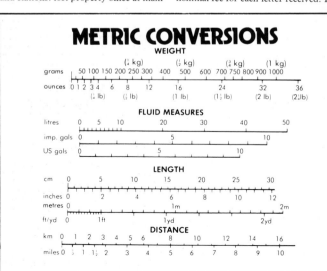

warding to Poste Restante elsewhere in Britain is free; forwarding to an address is chargeable.

Public holidays New Year's Day (1 Jan.; also 2 Jan. in Scotland); Good Friday and Easter Monday (movable dates); May Day (first Mon. in May); spring holiday (usually last Mon. in May); late summer holiday (usually last Mon. in Aug.; first Mon. in Scotland); Christmas Day (25 Dec.); Boxing Day (26 Dec.). Banks and most shops are closed on public holidays; most museums *etc*, are closed New Year's Day, Good Friday, Christmas and Boxing Day. Public transport services are reduced on all holidays.

Shopping Particularly good British buys are antiques, woollens, china, men's shoes, books, prints. Value Added Tax (VAT) is levied on most goods in Britain and on services, *e.g.* in hotels, restaurants. VAT on services cannot be reclaimed. VAT is not levied in the Channel Islands.

Visitors from countries other than some in the EEC will find it financially worthwhile to buy goods under retail export schemes (ask in relevant shops and take your passport), through which VAT relief may be obtained. Some visitors may have to pay tax in their own country if they receive VAT relief in Britain, and should exercise judgement based on knowledge of the tax rates in their own countries.

Telephone and telegrams Public telephones are found on the street, in post offices and in most pubs and restaurants. Pay boxes take 10p coins. In city centres, railway stations and airports new blue payphones (which take all UK coins except 1p) and cardphones are in use. Phone cards – in 40, 100 and 200 units – can be bought at post offices and shops displaying the green cardphone sign. Most inland calls can be dialled direct. Each town/area has a code of two, three or four figures to be dialled before the actual number. This code is omitted when dialling within the town/area but must be used when phoning from outside a town/area. Codes are displayed in telephone booths or in the information pages of the telephone directory.

International calls are cheaper between 2000–0800 hours and all day Sat. and Sun. Pay boxes can be used only for calls to Europe and North Africa. Overseas telegrams can, however, be dictated from a pay box by dialling 100 (193 in London) and dictating the message to the operator who will then state the amount of money to be inserted.

For emergency calls (free) for police, fire or ambulance dial 999 and state the service you require.

For telephoning inland telemessages,

dial as indicated in the telephone directory or contact the operator (100).

Time In winter Britain operates on Greenwich Mean Time, but British Summer Time operates from end March–end Oct., when clocks are put forward one hour. In general, USA and Canada are approximately five hours behind Greenwich Mean Time while Europe is approximately one hour ahead. Remember the difference in time zones when making overseas calls, and adjust your watch on arrival and departure.

Tipping No fixed rules or tariffs; the following is intended only as a guide to customary practice.

Hotels: Many hotel bills include a service charge, usually $10-12\frac{1}{2}\%$, but in some larger hotels, 15%. Where a service charge is not included, it is customary to divide 10–15% of the bill among the staff who have given good personal service.

Porterage: Depends on the size of baggage and distance carried, but usually 25p per suitcase.

Garage: It is not customary to tip unless some special service has been provided.

Taxis: 10–15% of the fare. When the driver helps you with your baggage, a larger tip is appreciated.

Theatre: The usherette at the theatre or cinema does not expect a tip.

Hairdressers: It is customary to give 5–10% depending on type of appointment and about 50p to the assistant who washes your hair.

Toilets Britain's public toilets are generally clean and hygienic. They are found at railway stations, in larger town centres and in large stores. Restaurants and pubs have toilets for customers. Facilities are scarce in small villages and country areas.

USEFUL ADDRESSES

(tel. nos in brackets)

Tourist Organizations

All the offices listed below welcome personal callers, except for those marked † (written enquiries only) and ††(written and telephone enquiries only). Most towns now have Information Centres. A list can be obtained from BTA offices in England and Tourist Information Centres.

†English Tourist Board, Thames Tower, Black's Rd, Hammersmith, London W6. Scottish Tourist Board, 19 Cockspur St, London SW1 (01-930 8661). Wales Tourist Board, 23 Maddox St, London W1 (01-409 0969).

London †London Visitor and Convention Bureau, Central Information Unit, 26, Grosvenor Gardens, SW1. Telephone Information Service: 01-730 3488. Personal callers only: National Tourist Information Centre, Victoria Station Forecourt, SW1; 4th Floor, Harrods Store, Brompton Rd, SW3; Ground Floor, Selfridges Store, Oxford St., W1; Information Centre, Heathrow Central Station, Heathrow Airport.

South East ††South East England Tourist Board, 1 Warwick Park, Tunbridge Wells, Kent (Tunbridge Wells (0892) 40766).

The South Southern Tourist Board, Town Hall Centre, Leigh Rd, Eastleigh, Hampshire SO5 4DE (Eastleigh (0703) 616027). **Isle of Wight** Isle of Wight Tourist Board, 21 High St., Newport, Isle of Wight (Isle of Wight (0983) 524343).

Channel Islands States of Jersey Tourist Committee, Weighbridge, St Helier, Jersey (Jersey (0534) 78000). States of Guernsey Tourist Board, PO Box 23, St Peter Port, Guernsey (Guernsey (0481) 23552). Tourism Committee, States Office, Alderney (Alderney (048 182) 2994). Herm Island Administrative Office, Herm Island, Via Guernsey (Herm 4 or Guernsey (0481) 22377). Sark Tourist Information Offices, Sark (Sark (048 183) 2345).

West Country West Country Tourist Board, Trinity Court, 37 Southernhay East, Exeter, Devon (Exeter (0392) 76351).

Wales Wales Tourist Board, Brunel House, 2 Fitzalan Rd, Cardiff CF2 1UY. (Cardiff (0222) 499909).

Heart of England ††Heart of England Tourist Board, PO Box 15, Worcester (Worcester (0905) 29511).

Thames and Chilterns Thames and Chilterns Tourist Board, 8 The Market Place, Abingdon, Oxfordshire (Abingdon (0235) 22711).

East Anglia ††East Anglia Tourist Board, 14 Museum St., Ipswich, Suffolk (Ipswich (0473) 214211).

The Shires ††East Midlands Tourist Board, Exchequergate, Lincoln (Lincoln (0522) 31521 and 31523).

Rose Counties ††North West Tourist Board – for Cheshire, Greater Manchester, Merseyside, Lancashire, High Peak area of Derbyshire – The Last Drop Village, Bromley Cross, Bolton (Bolton (0204) 591511). ††Yorkshire and Humberside Tourist Board – for North, South, West Yorkshire, Humberside – 312 Tadcaster Rd, York, North Yorkshire (York (0904) 707961). **Isle of Man** Isle of Man Tourist Board, 13 Victoria St., Douglas, Isle of Man (Douglas (0624) 74323).

The North †Cumbria Tourist Board, Ashleigh, Holly Road, Windermere, Cumbria. Northumbria Tourist Board – for Cleveland, Durham, Northumberland, Tyne & Wear – 9 Osborne Terrace, Newcastle upon Tyne (Newcastle (0632) 817744).

Scotland ††Scottish Tourist Board, 23 Ravelston Terrace, Edinburgh (031-332 2433). Personal callers and telephone enquiries: 5 Waverley Bridge, Edinburgh (031-332 6591); Prestwick Airport (Prestwick (0292) 77309). †Highlands and Islands Development Board, Bridge House, 27 Bank St., Inverness.

BTA Offices Overseas

Belgium Rue de la Montagne, 52 Bergstraat, B2 1000, Brussels (02/511.43.90) **Canada** 94 Cumberland St, Suite 600, Toronto, Ontario M5R 3N3 ((416)925-6326). **Denmark** Møntergade 3, DK-1116 Copenhagen K ((01) 12 07 93). **France** 6 Place Vêndome, 75001 Paris (296 47 60). **Italy** Via S. Eufemia 5, 00187 Rome (678.4998 or 678.5548). **Netherlands** Leidseplein 23, 1017 P5 Amsterdam ((020) 23 46 67). **Norway** Mariboes gt 11, 0183 Oslo 1 ((02) 41 1499). **Spain** Torre de Madrid 6/4, Plaza de España, Madrid 28008 ((91) 241 1396). **Sweden** For visitors: Malmskillnadsg 42, 1st Floor. For mail: Box 7293, S – 103 90 Stockholm (08-21 24 44). **Switzerland** Limmatquai 78, 8001 Zurich (01/47 42 77 or 47 42 97). **USA** 40 West 57th St, New York, NY 10019 ((212) 581 – 4700). Also : 612 South Flower St., Los Angeles, CA 90017 ((213) 623 – 8196). Also: John Hancock Center (Suite 3320), 875 North Michigan Ave, Chicago, Ill 60611 ((312) 787 – 0490). **West Germany** Neue Mainzer Str. 22, 6000 Frankfurt am Main 1 ((069) 2380711/12).

Miscellaneous Addresses

American Express: 6 Haymarket, London SW1; 17–19, Martineau Square, Birmingham; 54 Lord St, Liverpool; 139 Princes St., Edinburgh; 115 Hope St., Glasgow.
Automobile Association, Fanum House, Basingstoke, Hants.
British Rail Travel Centre, Lower Regent St., London SW1.
London Regional Transport Enquiry Offices: Piccadilly Circus, Oxford Circus, Heathrow Central, King's Cross, Euston, Victoria and St James's Park Underground Stations; British Rail Travel Office, Waterloo Station.
National Travel Express Coaches Enquiry Bureau, Victoria Coach Station, Buckingham Palace Rd, London SW1.
Thomas Cook has offices in all major cities – check in local telephone directory.

LONDON

Red buses, St Paul's Cathedral, Hyde Park, Harrods . . . just a handful of the images which evoke London. Yet even if you set out to visit all the traditional sights you'd only scratch the surface of this vast capital, which conceals as much as it reveals at first glance. And by the time you've discovered historic attractions like the Tower of London (over 900 years old), been shopping in the West End, seen a stage-show or play (perhaps at the National Theatre or Barbican Centre), you'll find there's still so much more to see and do . . .

London Past

There has been some kind of settlement beside the Thames for nearly 2000 years, and it was the Romans who first began to build a systematic communications network. In 1066 William the Conqueror swept into London, was crowned at Westminster, and drew up plans for a fortress – the Tower of London. Buildings increased and London spread westwards with the erection of a palace and an abbey at Westminster, and the setting up of smaller communities south of the river: Southwark was a pleasure centre, and the Globe Theatre was built there in 1599.

But when the Great Fire consumed London in 1666, four-fifths of the buildings were destroyed. A new city rose from the ashes, the reconstruction culminating in the completion of St Paul's Cathedral, in 1711. From then on the capital expanded rapidly with the population. Nelson's Column was erected in 1841, while the first London Underground railway lines were laid in 1863.

London Present

Today London covers about 1904 sq km/735 sq mi, extending for about 56 km/35 mi along the Thames and housing around 7,500,000 people. When coming to London, it's best to book ahead (see p. 17) and plan your stay. It makes more sense to take one area and explore the sights and activities there, rather than travelling to and fro across London – both time-consuming and expensive.

The best way to get to know the city is on foot. An excellent series of walks with guide/lecturer is organized by London Walks, 139 Conway Rd, Southgate N14 (tel: 01-882 2763). Alternatively if you're mapping your own route, arm yourself with the guide to London in this series and the London Tourist Board's latest official brochure. If you've only got a few days,

there are several day and half-day conducted coach tours: details from British Tourist Authority Offices overseas and London Visitor and Convention Bureaux (addresses on pp. 25–6).

As you start discovering London, you'll find that it is made up of a collection of 'villages', each with a distinct individuality and community. Central London has the villages of Soho, Covent Garden and Bloomsbury, then there's Hampstead and Highgate to the north and Dulwich on the river's south side.

Both historic and avant-garde, London is a city which preserves traditional treasures alongside its modern pleasures.

Eating Out Traditional food is now easier to find than a few years ago and you'll probably come across Bubble and Squeak (fried potatoes, onion, green vegetables) and Steak and Kidney Pudding, known to Cockneys as 'Kate and Sydney'. High street and market stalls sell cockles, mussels, whelks and prawns. Jellied eels are still popular, although eel and pie shops are now thinner on the ground than fish and chip shops – and even these are increasingly outnumbered by hamburger cafés, the quality of which varies considerably.

Department stores often have restaurants catering for shoppers, especially those with children, while many pubs offer reasonably priced snacks such as Shepherd's Pie, soup, sandwiches, salads and 'ploughmans' (bread, cheese, pickle).

Most hotels accept nonresidents for meals, but if your finances don't stretch to dinner at The Ritz, The Hilton, The Savoy or Claridges, then a fun thing to do is to go for afternoon tea (around 1600 hours).

Otherwise, variety is the spice of metropolitan eating, and the cuisine of most countries is represented. Soho with its Chinese, Italian, Greek and Indian restaurants is handy for sightseers, shoppers and theatre-goers, while the multitude of new cafés around Covent Garden cater for restaurant-goers in search of atmosphere as well as good food.

Festivals and Events Newspapers and posters advertise many events. Check with the London Visitor and Convention Bureau for more details and dates (tel: 01-730 3488).

Jan., London shops hold Sales; International Boat Show – Earl's Court; Chinese New Year celebrations – Soho. Feb., Cruft's Dog Show – Olympia. March/April, Antiques Fair – Chelsea Old Town Hall; Ideal Home Exhibition – Earl's Court; Oxford and Cambridge Boat Race – Putney to Mortlake. Easter Parade

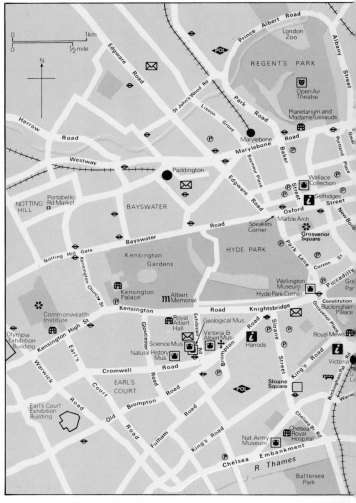

London Zoo

REGENT'S PARK

Open Air Theatre

Planetarium and Madame Tussauds

Prince Albert Road

Albany

Street

Great

Portland Place

Edgware Road

St John's Wood Rd

Lisson Grove

Park Road

Marylebone

Marylebone Road

Baker Street

Harrow

Road

Westway

Paddington

Edgware Road

Seymour Place

Wallace Collection

Selfridges

Oxford Street

New Bond

NOTTING HILL

Portobello Rd Market

BAYSWATER

Speakers Corner

Marble Arch

Grosvenor Square

Bayswater

Road

HYDE PARK

Park Lane

Curzon St

Notting Hill Gate

Kensington Church St

Kensington Gardens

Wellington Museum

Hyde Park Corner

Piccadilly

Green Park

Constitution

Kensington Palace

Albert Memorial

Kensington

Road

Knightsbridge

Buckingham Palace

Commonwealth Institute

Royal Albert Hall

Geological Mus

Grosvenor Place

Royal Mews

Olympia Exhibition Building

Kensington High St

Gloucester Road

Science Mus

Natural History Mus

Victoria & Albert Mus

Exhibition Rd

Brompton

Harrods

Sloane Street

Victoria

Earl's Court Road

Warwick Road

Cromwell Road

EARL'S COURT

Old Brompton Road

Fulham Road

King's Road

Sloane Square

Buckingham Pal Rd

Warw

Earl's Court Exhibition Building

Nat Army Museum

Chelsea Royal Hospital

Chelsea Br Rd

King's Road

Chelsea Embankment

R. Thames

Battersea Park

Temple Church

Royal Courts of Justice

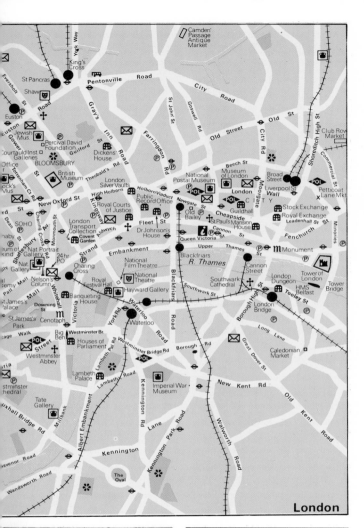

Lincoln's Inn Fields

Royal Opera House

– Battersea Park; Hampstead Heath fair. 21 April, Queen's Birthday – gun salutes from Hyde Park and the Tower; 23 April, Shakespeare's birthday service – Southwark Cathedral. May, Summer Art Exhibition – Royal Academy; Chelsea Flower Show – Royal Hospital Grounds. Sat. nearest 11 June, Trooping the Colour ceremony from Buckingham Palace; June/July, Wimbledon Lawn Tennis Championships. July–Sept., Henry Wood Promenade Concerts – Albert Hall. July, Royal Tournament – Earl's Court; Royal International Horse Show – Wembley. Aug., Notting Hill West Indian Carnival. 15 Sept., Battle of Britain Day – RAF fly over London. Oct., Horse of the Year Show – Wembley; Trafalgar Day – service and parade, Nelson's Column. Early Nov., veteran car run to Brighton from Hyde Park Corner; State Opening of Parliament by Queen; 5 Nov., Guy Fawkes' Day – fireworks in many areas; Sun. nearest 11 Nov., Remembrance Day ceremony – Cenotaph, Whitehall; Sat. nearest 12 Nov., Lord Mayor's Show – Procession from Guildhall to Law Courts. Nov./Dec., London Film Festival – National Film Theatre. 26–28 Dec., Westminster Carol Services.

Shopping Around Most shops open Mon.-Sat. 0900–1730 with late opening to 1900 or 2000 on Wed. (Knightsbridge) or Thurs. (Oxford Street area). Some shops close Wed. or Thurs. afternoon outside Central London.

Oxford Street is the shoppers' mecca, lined with department stores and chain shops (middle-range prices). At its east end junction with Tottenham Court Road tube station, turn south into Charing Cross Road for Foyles bookstore and new and second-hand bookshops; turn north up Tottenham Court Road for reasonably priced hi-fi, TV and electrical goods, and for Habitat and Heal's (modern living).

Oxford Street is over 1½km/1mi long with two Marks & Spencers (noted for good quality at reasonable prices). In the middle is Oxford Circus, to the south of which lie half-timbered Liberty and Co. (textiles and furnishings) and pedestrianized Carnaby Street, strictly for trendies. Bond Street (chic and expensive), with famous Aspreys (luxury goods), links Oxford Street to Piccadilly, where you'll find Fortnum & Mason, London's finest grocer, Hatchards (books), and Simpsons (high-class department store).

From Piccadilly, pick up a no. 14, 19 or 22 bus to take you to Harrods and the Scotch House in the exclusive shopping area of Knightsbridge and Brompton Road. A walk down Sloane Street brings you to Sloane Square and King's Road,

vivid with promenading trend-setters on Saturday afternoons. Fashion boutiques at the top end melt into antique shops further along. Fulham Road, parallel to King's Road, has interesting specialized shops and plenty of eating-places.

Covent Garden, WC2, with its lively shops and stalls housed in the original market building, is a nucleus area; pavement cafes and street entertainment are an added bonus to shopping.

For alternative shopping, visit Bayswater park-railings on Sunday morning (paintings, knick-knacks) and the markets: antiques at Portobello St, W11 (Mon.–Sat.); Camden Passage, N1 (Wed. and Sat.) and Bermondsey's New Caledonian Market, Tower Bridge Rd, SE1. Most famous of all is Petticoat Lane general street market at Middlesex St., E1 (best Sun. morning). Berwick St., W1 (Mon.–Sat.) sells mainly fruit and vegetables, while Brixton Market, SW9 has traditional West Indian food. Auctions at Sotheby's, Christie's and Phillips are fun to attend and many items are within reach of modest collectors (daily newspapers give details).

Entertainment London is rightly renowned as the world's leading centre for live theatre, and it offers hundreds of other nightly entertainments – highbrow and lowbrow, established and fringe. London's evening paper, *The Standard* gives details of theatre, opera and cinema, while the whole range of entertainments is listed comprehensively with potted reviews in *Time Out* magazine, published every Thursday. The listings include local films, late-night movies, all types of theatre, classical music, opera, concerts, dance, jazz, rock, folk, ballet, poetry readings, children's events – even political demonstrations and 'jumble' sales (second-hand bargains). Another magazine, *What's On*, gives wider coverage to nightclubs and is aimed more at tourists.

Excursions Greenwich, SE10. Well worth a day-long visit, especially for the **National Maritime Museum**. In front of the Observatory is the zero meridian from which Greenwich Mean Time is calculated. By the pier are Sir Francis Chichester's round-the-world yacht, *Gipsy Moth IV*, and the tea clipper, *Cutty Sark*, while a boat-tow will take visitors to see the futuristic Thames Barrier.

Hampton Court (19km/21mi SW of London). Hampton Court Palace was built by Cardinal Wolsey in the 16th century, extended by Henry VIII (five of his wives lived there) and part reconstructed by Wren in the 18th century. The State Apartments on the upper floor contain priceless paintings, furniture and tapestries. The Great Hall on the north side has a superb hammerbeam roof. Beautiful gardens include the unique maze and a 16th-century tennis court.

Children's London

A special phone number (01-246 8007) gives details of events for children day by day. **Travelling around** If you are under 16 you pay only a flat-rate for a ticket on a red bus, no matter how far you travel. More savings with a Red Bus Rover Ticket which allows unlimited travel during one day. You must be under 14 to qualify for a cheap ticket on the Underground. **Entertainment** Saturday children's plays are presented regularly at the Theatre Royal, Stratford East (tel: 01-534 0310) and the Unicorn Theatre, 6 Great Newport St., WC2 (tel: 01-836 3334). The Little Angel Marionette Theatre, Islington, N1 also caters specifically for children. **Shopping** Britain's biggest toyshop is Hamleys, Regent St., W1; Selfridges and Harrods also have good toy departments. **Outdoors** Regents Park Zoo, NW1; Battersea Park adventure playground; Hampstead Heath model-boat pond; Club Row (Sclater St.), E1 – Sun. morning pets market. **Collections** Most of London's museums will interest children as much as adults – these are just a few suggestions: Bethnal Green Museum of Childhood, Cambridge Heath Rd, E2 (toys); Madame Tussaud's, Marylebone Rd, NW1 (waxworks); Planetarium, Marylebone Rd, NW1 (sky and stars); Postal Museum, King Edward St., EC1 (worldwide stamps); Pollock's Toy Museum, 1 Scala St, W1; London Dungeon, 34 Tooley St., SE1 (waxworks, particularly medieval torture); HMS *Belfast*, Symon's Wharf, Vine Lane, SE1 (last of the Royal Navy's big gun cruisers); Dickens' House, 48 Doughty St., WC1 (Dickens' mementos); London Toy and Model Museum, 23 Craven Hill, W2; London Transport Collection, Old Flower Hall, Covent Garden, WC2; Royal Mews, Buckingham Palace Rd, SW1 (royal horses and carriages).

Traditional London

The London Visitor and Convention Bureau (tel: 01-730 3488) has details of all opening times.
Banqueting House, Whitehall, SW1. The only important surviving part of Whitehall Palace, built for James I in 1622.
Big Ben, Parliament Square, SW1 (exterior only).
Buckingham Palace, The Mall, SW1 (exterior only). The Queen's official London home. Changing the Guard takes place outside at 1130 daily in summer (except in bad weather); alternate days in winter.
The *Queen's Gallery*, Buckingham Palace Rd, SW1. Art from the Royal Collection.
Chelsea Royal Hospital, Royal Hospital Rd, Chelsea, SW3. Home of the red-coated Chelsea Pensioners.
Downing Street, off Whitehall, SW1 (exterior only). Prime Minister's official home is No. 10.
Fleet Street, EC4. Hub of the newspaper world. Also in the area are the Royal Courts of Justice (Law Courts), Ye Olde Cheshire Cheese pub, El Vino's Wine Bar and Dr Johnson's house.
Guildhall, King St., Cheapside, EC2. Civic hall where City functions take place.
Houses of Parliament, Westminster, SW1.
Kensington Palace State Apartments, Kensington Gardens, W8. Royal apartments where Queen Victoria and Queen Mary were born with *objets d'art* and Court Dress Collections.
Mansion House, Bank, EC4. (exterior only). The Lord Mayor of London's official residence.
Monument, near King William St., EC3. Commemorates the Great Fire of 1666.
Old Bailey, Newgate St., EC4. The Central Criminal Court: Public Gallery open weekdays.
Public Record Office, Kew. National records, dating from the Norman Conquest, including the Domesday Book.
Royal Exchange, Bank, EC3.
St James's Palace, St James's St., SW1 (exterior only).
St Paul's Cathedral, Ludgate Hill, EC4.
Stock Exchange, Old Broad St., EC2. Visitors' Gallery open weekdays.
Tower of London, Tower Hill, EC3. Armouries and uniforms; Crown Jewels.
Trafalgar Square with Nelson's Column.
Westminster Abbey, Parliament Square, SW1. Scene of the coronations of almost all English monarchs since William the Conqueror.

Museums and Galleries

The London Visitor and Convention Bureau has details of all opening times and admission charges (tel: 01-730 3488).
British Museum, Great Russell St., WC1. History, art and archaeology.
Cabinet War Rooms, Great George St., SW1 includes Sir Winston Churchill's private War Office.
Commonwealth Institute, 230 Kensington High St., W8. All aspects of Commonwealth countries.
Courtauld Institute, Woburn Square, WC1. Impressionist paintings (soon to move – tel: 01-387 0370 for new address).
Geffrye Museum, Kingsland Rd, E2. Furnished period rooms.
Geological Museum, Exhibition Rd, SW7.

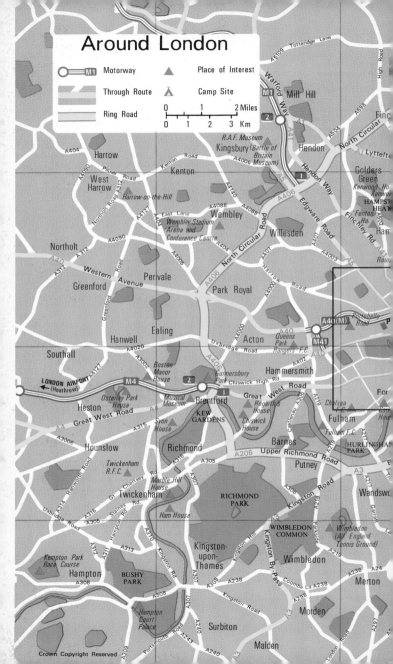

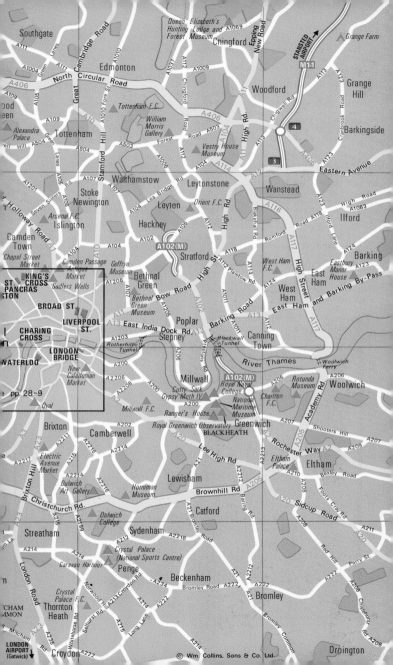

Earth's development; famous gemstone collection.

Hayward Gallery, South Bank, SE1. Major art exhibitions.

Hogarth House, Hogarth Lane, Great West Rd, W4. Home of 18th-century artist William Hogarth, containing mementos.

Horniman Museum, 100 London Rd, Forest Hill, SE23. Ethnographical and zoological specimens; musical instruments.

Imperial War Museum, Lambeth Rd, SE1. Aspects of both world wars.

Jewish Museum, Woburn House, Tavistock Square, WC1. Religious history of the Jewish people.

Kenwood House, Hampstead Lane, NW3. Fine paintings and period furnishings.

London Silver Vaults, 53 Chancery Lane, WC2. Modern and antique silverware.

Madame Tussauds, Marylebone Rd NW1. Wax effigies of the famous.

Museum of London, London Wall, EC2. Comprehensive collection illustrating London's 2000-year history.

Museum of Mankind, 6 Burlington Gardens, W1. Tribal and folk arts and crafts of all the world's peoples.

National Army Museum, Royal Hospital, Chelsea, SW3. Exhibits from 1485–1914.

National Gallery, Trafalgar Square, WC2. Chief European schools of painting from 13th century to 1900.

National Portrait Gallery, St Martin's Place, WC2. Portraits of famous British people from Tudor times on. (Apart from the royal family, there are no portraits of anyone living.)

Natural History Museum, Cromwell Rd, SW7. Animals, insects, plants, minerals and meteorites.

Percival David Foundation, 53 Gordon Square, WC1. Chinese ceramics.

RAF Museum, Grahame Park Way, Aerodrome Rd, NW9. Aircraft history and development.

Royal Academy of Arts, Burlington House, Piccadilly, W1. Major art exhibitions.

Science Museum, Exhibition Rd, SW7. History and development of science and industry.

Tate Gallery, Millbank, SW1. British paintings of all periods, modern foreign painting, modern sculpture.

Victoria and Albert Museum, Cromwell Rd, SW7. Decorative arts and crafts.

Wallace Collection, Manchester Square, W1. Mainly French 18th-century paintings, sculpture, furniture, porcelain.

Wellington Museum, Apsley House, Hyde Park Corner, W1. Pictures, porcelain and silver of the first Duke of Wellington.

Whitechapel Art Gallery, 80 Whitechapel High St., E1. Modern art.

Houses of Parliament

THE SOUTH EAST

The White Cliffs of Dover are, perhaps, England's most evocative landmark, they also guard Britain's south-easterly entry point. Because this corner has always been an important gateway, it has suffered its share of strife over the centuries. The Romans came ashore here, leaving traces of their sojourn (Pevensey Castle, between Eastbourne and Hastings, for example), while the Norman invasion culminated in the Battle of Hastings – Battle Abbey marks the spot where the English king, Harold, was slain.

In the 13th century, a group of five ports, known as the Cinque Ports, were granted special privileges and exercised coastal jurisdiction. To the original ports of Hastings, Sandwich, Dover, Romney and Hythe, two more were added in the 14th century – Rye and Winchelsea.

Henry VIII, always concerned about French invaders, erected a coastal defence chain which included castles at Deal and Walmer. In the 19th century, threats of Napoleonic attack caused the construction of two-story gun turrets called Martello Towers (particularly prominent between Dungeness and Lydd). Some 'gentlemen' had more commercial causes in mind when they crept ashore at night: smuggling was rife in the 18th century and Rye, Dymchurch, Hawkhurst and Alfriston are all old smuggling centres.

During the 18th century, royal patronage encouraged the growth of seaside watering-places and these developed into today's sparkling array of south-coast resorts, behind which spread the South Downs: miles of farmland, hills and woods, with the South Downs Way, a long-distance footpath stretching from Eastbourne to the cathedral city of Chichester.

In the area of Kent known as The Weald, villages are either built from a characteristic mix of weatherboard and red brick, or are half-timbered like Biddenden and Chiddingstone. Worth a visit are Goudhurst with its weatherboarded and tile-hung houses, Cranbrook, a cloth-making centre 500 years ago, and the small Elizabethan town of Mayfield. Tenterden, another traditional wool town, is the chief station on the preserved Kent and East Sussex steam railway.

Not for nothing has the Kent countryside been dubbed 'The Garden of England', and the conical-roofed oast houses (see them around Maidstone) used for drying hops indicate that the area is noted for hop-growing as well as fruit and other garden produce. Faversham is a good touring centre and the best time to come is April or May when the orchards and woodlands are clouded with blossom.

The North Downs swing across Kent into Surrey, and curving across the hills from Dover to Farnham is another long-distance footpath, the North Downs Way, which in places merges with the traditional Pilgrims' Way leading to Canterbury Cathedral.

Surrey is rightly proud of its delightful villages, tucked away among the woods, heaths and commons, with poetic names like Friday Street, Abinger, Holmbury St Mary, Shere and Chiddingfold. Surrey also has several significant places: Epsom with its world-famous annual Derby horse race; Runnymede (3km/2mi W of Staines) where the historic Magna Carta was signed; and Haslemere, noted for its annual July festival of early music.

Fruit and Hops Lamb from Sussex and Kent is world-famous and goes into hot-pots (casseroles) or is roasted with mint. Other delicacies come ashore: Whitstable oysters, Dover sole, crabs, mullet and whiting.

This rich farming area yields plenty of fruit which is either preserved or made into puddings such as Sussex Pond Pudding, Plum Duff (an early 19th-century recipe) and Gipsy Bread made with black treacle. There are savoury puddings too, like Ashdown Partridge Pudding – a mixture of game and meat dating back to medieval times. Fruit also features in biscuits and buns here – Sussex Plum Heavies, Brighton Rocks and Oast Cakes.

Hops are used in local recipes to flavour sauces for chicken and fish, although their more traditional use is in producing beer. Light and very 'hoppy' beer comes from Shepherd Neame Brewery in Faversham;

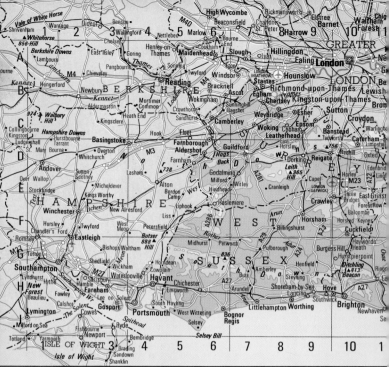

other breweries include King and Barnes at Horsham and Harveys at Lewes.

Markets especially good for fruit and vegetables include those at Ashford, Canterbury, Faversham, Maidstone, Tonbridge, Guildford, Farnham, Hailsham and Chichester.

Festivals and Events March, Garden Show – Brighton. Mid-April, Easter Egg Hunt – Leeds Castle. Early May, Leith Hill Music Festival – Dorking; International Folk Festival – Eastbourne; Brighton Festival; mid-May, Chichester Festival Theatre Season; Brighton Boat Show; late May, Goodwood Race Meeting; Surrey County Show – Guildford; International Showjumping – Hickstead. May–June, Dickens Festival – Rochester. May–Aug., Glyndebourne Festival. June, South of England Agricultural Show – Ardingly. Early June, World Custard Pie Throwing Championship – Maidstone; late June, Broadstairs Dickens Festival. Early July, Dover Carnival; July, Maidstone River Festival; Mid-July, Kent County Show – Detling; late July, Haslemere Festival; Battle Festival; Aug; Town Criers' Championship – Hastings.

Early Aug., Broadstairs Folk Week; late Aug., Arundel Festival; Medieval jousting – Chilham Castle. Sept–Oct.; Canterbury Festival. 5 Nov., Lewes Bonfire Celebrations.

Brighton   H10

East Sussex (pop. 234,437) This seaside town was made famous in the 18th century by the Prince Regent, later George IV. Before the days of royal patronage, Brighton was a fishing village, and in the 17th century the narrow byways called 'The Lanes' were lined with fishermen's cottages (today many are antique shops). The onion-domed Royal Pavilion was the Prince Regent's seaside home. This dazzling and exotic palace was built by Henry Holland and John Nash in the style of the mogul palaces and mosques in India; the interior is lavishly furnished in Chinese style. Brighton Museum and Art Gallery contains exhibits of Sussex folk life, while Preston Manor displays period furniture, china and silver in a Georgian house. Volks Railway, Britain's first electric railway (opened 1883), runs along the seafront.

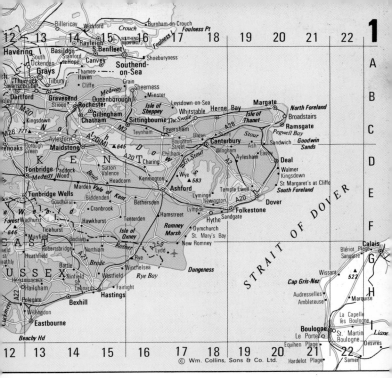

Broadstairs C20

Kent (pop. 20,048) Broadstairs has many connections with the Victorian novelist, **Charles Dickens**, and each June the inhabitants dress up in Dickensian costume to pay tribute to the great author in a Dickens' Festival. The Dickens House Museum, immortalized in the novel *David Copperfield* as the home of Betsy Trotwood, contains Dickens' letters and possessions. Bleak House is also notable for its associations with Dickens. Broadstairs has the normal English seaside attractions of pier, promenade, Punch and Judy shows and donkey-rides on the beach, while other famous Kent resorts offering similar attractions are **Margate**, 5km/3mi NW, with its huge Amusement Park and **Ramsgate**, 3km/2mi S, with its smart marina and sandy beaches.

Canterbury C18

Kent (pop. 33,176) The history of this ancient city spans 2000 years and is still marvellously evident. Canterbury Cathedral, mother church of Anglicans throughout the world, dates from Norman times. For several centuries after the murder of Thomas à Becket inside the cathedral in 1170, his shrine was the destination of countless pilgrims. The 13th- and 14th-century town walls, built on Roman foundations, still stand in short stretches, although only one of the seven original gates remains as it was – West Gate, which now houses a museum devoted to Canterbury's history.

Other places to see are 12th-century Eastbridge (St Thomas') Hospital; the ruins of St Augustine's Abbey; and the restored 14th-century Poor Priests' Hospital, now containing displays which take the form of a time walk through Canterbury's history from the first town under the Romans to the present day, and including a collection of early treasures such as Anglo-Saxon gold. Part of a Roman pavement can be seen in Butchery Lane, while more Roman and Anglo-Saxon finds are housed in the Royal Museum. The Marlowe Theatre is the main venue for the annual Canterbury Festival. You can visit **Chilham** with its castle 10km/6mi SW; also **Faversham**, 13km/8mi W, which has over 400 buildings of historic importance.

River Arun and castle, Arundel

Chichester   H5

West Sussex (pop. 20,649) The Roman
street-plan of this historic town has been
preserved, along with much elegant Georgian architecture. Chichester Cathedral,
founded in 1075, remains largely un-
altered since the 12th century except for
the spire, and is noted for its interior
medieval carvings. Chichester harbour
merits exploration on foot; see also the
Yacht Basin's lively marina. The Summer
Festival attracts visitors from all over the
world, as does the Festival Theatre's
summer season of plays.

Chichester is a good base for exploring
interesting places nearby: **Fishbourne
Roman Palace** with its mosaic pavements 1½km/1mi W; 18th-century **Goodwood House** and racecourse 6km/4mi N;
Arundel with its Georgian houses and
castle 16km/10mi E; and the jolly seaside
resort of **Bognor Regis** 10km/6mi SE.

Dorking   D8

Surrey (pop. 22,530) This old coaching
and market town is surrounded by the
rolling, grassy hills of the North Downs.
From Dorking you can easily reach pretty
villages like Gomshall and Friday Street,
and beauty spots like Leith Hill and Box
Hill (named after its box-tree woods).
Dorking itself has a 400-year-old inn and
is noted for antiques and music festivals.
The Regency mansion, **Polesden Lacey**,
5km/3mi NW, was built in 1824; open-air
theatre is presented in the grounds in
summer.

Epsom, 13km/8mi NE, was established as a fashionable spa in the mid 18th
century; some of its 17th- and 18th-
century houses survive. Horse racing,

introduced by James I in the 17th century
as a courtly diversion, became a permanent fixture from 1779 when the Derby
was first run.

Dover   E20

Kent (pop. 34,395) One of the original
Cinque Ports, it is now England's busiest
passenger port. Traces of the Roman
settlement are evident in The Painted
House and England's earliest lighthouse;
other historic reminders include a Saxon
church and Dover Castle, built by the
Normans using Roman foundation
stones. The Town Hall's central core
consists of a 13th-century guest house, the
Maison Dieu, now containing historic
armour.

Good coastal walks can be taken to
Folkestone, 10km/6mi SW, and to
Walmer 11km/7mi NE, passing St
Margaret's Bay. Henry VIII built
Walmer Castle in the 16th century as part
of his coastal defence plan; its sister castle
is at **Deal**, 13km/8mi NE of Dover.

Sandwich, 16km/10mi N, also one of
the original Cinque Ports until its harbour
silted up, has a remarkable number of
historic buildings including the Barbican
and Quay, Fisher's Gate and several
almshouses.

Eastbourne   I13

East Sussex (pop. 70,921) The 175m/
575ft high cliffs of Beachy Head shelter
this large seaside resort, while flower
gardens, a pier and bandstand enliven its
5km/3mi seafront. One of the 19th-
century Martello Towers now displays
defence methods and equipment from the
Napoleonic period. Lifeboats (from the

White Cliffs of Dover

Derby Day on Epsom Downs

earliest times) can be seen in the Royal National Lifeboat Museum, while collections of 19th- and 20th-century British paintings are shown in the Towner Art Gallery, itself a Georgian manor house. From Eastbourne you might explore pretty local villages at **Eastdean**, 6km/4mi SW, **Alfriston** 11km/7mi NW, and **Wilmington** 8km/5mi NW, with its giant chalk figure cut into the South Downs hillside.

Folkestone   E19
Kent (pop. 43,801) Old narrow streets wind down to the original fishermen's quarter near the harbour of this popular seaside town which doubles as an important cross-Channel port. You can take several pleasant walks in and around the town, one of which – a promenade called The Leas – runs along the clifftops 60m/200ft above sea level.

Hythe, 8km/5mi W, is one terminal of the Romney, Hythe and Dymchurch Light Railway. This daily passenger steam service puffs 22km/14mi across Romney Marsh to Dungeness and is the world's only main-line in miniature, with locomotives one-third of normal size.

Guildford   D7
Surrey (pop. 57,213) This historic town is the county town of Surrey and boasts a wealth of old buildings: St Mary's Saxon church; Norman castle ruins; 16th-century grammar school; 17th-century almshouses and guildhall in the cobbled High Street. In contrast, modern developments include The Cathedral of the Holy Spirit (consecrated 1961); the recent University of Surrey; and the Yvonne

Arnaud Theatre overlooking the River Wey.

Godalming, 6km/4mi SW, a small town of 16th–18th-century houses, is set in the Wey Valley near beauty spots like the Hog's Back and Devil's Punch Bowl. Winkworth Arboretum with its shrubs, rare trees and massed bluebells is close by.

Hastings   H15
East Sussex (pop. 72,410) Once a fishing village and later one of the Cinque Ports, Hastings is now a modern seaside resort spreading westwards into St Leonards. The remains of the clifftop castle are Norman, while St Clement's Caves, cut into the slopes of West Hill and covering over 1·6 hectares/4 acres, are associated with smugglers. A former fishermen's church now houses the Fishermen's Museum, containing items of local interest, including the last of Hastings' luggers built for sail.

Herstmonceux Castle, 16km/10mi NW, has been the home of the Royal Greenwich Observatory since 1957. Herstmonceux itself is the home of the traditional Sussex trug (basket) industry. The Battle of Hastings, in which William the Conqueror defeated the English king, Harold, in 1066, took place at the town of **Battle** 10km/6mi NW; the Norman invader erected Battle Abbey to celebrate his victory.

Lewes   H11
East Sussex (pop. 14,159) A thousand years of history have left their mark on the county town of Sussex, in the shape of a ruined Norman castle, a jumble of medieval streets and various Georgian

buildings. Museums to visit are the archaeological collection at Barbican House and the folk museum in Anne of Cleves House. The latter dates from the 16th century, and was given to Anne by Henry VIII after their divorce. Bull House Restaurant was once the house of the 18th-century pamphleteer, **Tom Paine**, who used to meet fellow radicals at the White Hart Hotel, also in the High Street. **Glyndebourne**, 5km/3mi E, is internationally famous for its opera season which opens in May.

Maidstone   D14

Kent (pop. 70,987) Maidstone is a busy market town (market-day is Tuesday) and the county town of Kent; also a centre for hop-growing and has a flourishing brewing industry. Chillington Manor, a Tudor mansion, houses the Museum and Art Gallery while an impressive carriage collection is contained in the 14th-century Tithe Barn. **Allington Castle**, 1½km/1mi W, is a 13th-century moated stronghold, once the home of Tudor poet Thomas Wyatt. **Leeds Castle**, 6km/4mi SE, is also moated; it dates from 857 and was particularly favoured by the medieval Queens of England. The most recent restoration was in the 1920s when the present collection of art, furniture and tapestries was assembled.

Midhurst   G6

West Sussex (pop. 2169) Brick and timber-framed 16th- and 18th-century houses characterize this attractive market town, which is further enhanced by the market square, the pond, the old grammar school which has associations with the Victorian novelist H.G. Wells. On the edge of town are the ruins of Cowdray House, built in 1520.

The country town of **Petworth**, with its narrow streets, tea-rooms and antique shops, lies 10km/6mi E. The picture gallery is worth seeing at Petworth House, a 17th–19th-century mansion, while, 8km/5mi S is **Bignor Roman Villa**, occupied much earlier – in the 2nd and 4th centuries. Despite its age, it still retains fine mosaic pavements.

Rochester   B14

Kent (pop. 55,519) This cathedral city, port and commercial centre figured in the novels of 19th-century author, **Charles Dickens**. You can walk round the many places associated with him: the Guildhall Museum, the Six Poor Travellers' house and the Swiss chalet he used as a garden-study in the grounds of his last home at Gad's Hill. The Dickens Centre at Eastgate House depicts the writer's life and times as well as his characters and novels.

Rochester's present cathedral, standing on the site of the original Saxon church, was largely built in the 12th century. Inside, a series of bishops' tombs date from over seven centuries ago. Around the cathedral are the remains of former monastic buildings, the ruined chapter house and cloisters. The castle was built shortly after 1066, but only the keep – built in Henry II's reign – remains.

Carmelite friars restored 13th-century **Aylesford Priory**, 8km/5mi, now containing sculpture and ceramics by contemporary artists.

Rye   G16

East Sussex (pop. 4449) Once a flourishing seaport, Rye is now 3km/2mi inland but linked to the sea by the River Rother. Medieval, Tudor and Georgian houses grace the hilly streets, many of which are cobbled. Rye's largest medieval building is the Mermaid Inn, a former smugglers' haunt. The Town Hall dates from 1742, while 18th-century Lamb House is home to the novelist **Henry James**. Ypres Tower, built in the 13th century as a fort, houses a local history museum.

Romney Marsh, which lies north east of Rye, has a wealth of lovely churches. One of the most beautiful is at Brookland 8km/5mi NE; others include St George's at Ivychurch, 13km/8mi NE, with a lookout post on the tower, which was used to espy French raiders; St Clements at Old Romney, 13km/8mi NE; and All Saints at Lydd, 11km/7mi E.

Tunbridge Wells   E13

Kent (pop. 44,612) Set amid wooded Kentish countryside, Tunbridge Wells became a fashionable spa in the 17th century. It was Queen Anne's favourite resort and by her time, the Pantiles – a paved, tree-shaded walk in the older part of town – had already been laid out. You can picture the town in bygone days by inspecting old prints and local mementos in the Museum and Art Gallery.

Penshurst Place, 8km/5mi NW, the magnificent birthplace of the Elizabethan courtier and poet, Sir Philip Sidney, contains an impressive collection of armour; see also the huge Barons Hall, built 1341, and the great State Rooms.

Hever Castle, 11km/7mi NW, was the home of Anne Boleyn, Henry VIII's second wife and mother of Queen Elizabeth I. While Hever is encircled by a moat, **Sissinghurst Castle**, 19km/12mi E, is surrounded by the beautiful gardens created by the writer Victoria Sackville-West and her husband, Sir Harold Nicolson.

THE SOUTH

The coastline of Hampshire and Dorset, in common with that of Kent and Sussex further east, has always been an important gateway into Britain. The Romans built a castle at Portchester, north of Portsmouth, while the Saxons, coming here first to fight, then to trade and settle, made Winchester their capital city. With trade came the ports – Southampton, Gosport, Poole and Portsmouth – which still retain their historic interest. You can tour Southampton docks by boat and marvel at the size of the elegant liners which call there – Cunard's *QE2* and the P&O ship SS *Canberra*. Nelson's HMS *Victory* is dry-docked at Portsmouth, where signs of the Navy can be seen everywhere – from white-hatted sailors to street names like Gunwharf Lane.

This coastline falls into three distinct categories: from the holiday centre of Hayling Island (linked to the mainland by road bridge) it is a shipping coast. But beyond Southampton there is a stretch of marshy, undeveloped shoreline, excellent for pastimes like fishing, bird-watching and yachting. Then come the seaside resorts – Bournemouth, with its splendid sands and scented pine woods, close to the holiday towns of Christchurch, Poole and Swanage.

Opposite this indented coastline, the Isle of Wight is 'anchored' 6km/4mi away; it is easily reached by ferry or hydrofoil (see p. 15). Perhaps the Island's most famous landmark is the three huge off-shore rocks called The Needles. Inland, thatched villages complement the charm of seaside resorts like Shanklin and Ventnor, characterized by their air of bygone Victorian days.

A broad stretch of water, The Solent, divides the Isle of Wight from the mainland. Southampton Water cuts right up into the country and narrows into the River Test which flows by the Norman abbey of Romsey, founded in the 10th century, and still a lovely spot. Further north lies Winchester, from which the first Roman roads radiated. Under King Alfred, who ruled from 871–899, Winchester flourished as a great centre of learning. Even today, glimpses of English history from earliest times can be enjoyed in this ancient city, so famous for its medieval cathedral and public school.

Peaceful downland traced by rural lanes characterizes the southern countryside with its old market towns such as Wareham and Wimborne Minster, and unspoiled villages like Titchfield, in the south, and the Wallops in the north west –

Over Wallop, Middle Wallop and Nether Wallop which has early wall-paintings in its solemn little church.

The New Forest, once a royal hunting ground, is one of England's largest unenclosed areas and spreads through much of Hampshire. Although it is quite accessible by car, it's more pleasing to explore the remoter parts on foot. There are some deer here still, but you are more likely to see the half-wild ponies which wander freely. One much-visited spot is the stone at Stoney Cross in Canterton Glen near the A31 – a memorial to William Rufus (William II) who was killed by an arrow while hunting in the Forest.

Another memorial stone, north east of Wickham at Hambledon, opposite the Bat and Ball Inn, commemorates an event dear to the heart of most Englishmen: cricket, as we know it today, started here in 1774.

Details of Channel Islands are on p. 46.

Wine and Watercress Although the New Forest still provides a little venison, local recipes make more use of pork and bacon, which once came from pigs roaming the Forest. Hampshire Haslet, for example, is a baked mixture of bread and minced pork.

Watercress grows well here and is featured in stuffing for lamb and chicken, watercress soup and watercress sauce to enhance freshwater fish. Local fish include the trout and salmon caught in the Rivers Test and Itchen, as well as plaice and flounder from Poole Bay.

Vine-planting, introduced by the Romans, is currently enjoying a revival: wine from vineyards in Hampshire and the Isle of Wight is popular; so is local beer from breweries producing a variety of traditional ales, including Bourne Valley Brewery at Andover, Burt and Company, Ventnor, and the Ringwood Brewery at Ringwood.

Markets selling food include Christchurch, Eastleigh, Portsmouth, Ringwood, Southampton, Wareham and Winchester.

Festivals and Events Easter, Sandown Carnival. May. Winchester Folk Festival; Crab Fayre – Ventnor. June, Smuggling Pageant – Ventnor; Beaulieu Country Sports and Crafts Fair; mid-June, Round the Island (Isle of Wight) Yacht Race. July, Southampton Show; Royal Isle of Wight County Show – Cowes; Southsea Carnival; New Forest Show. July/Aug., Swanage Regatta and Carnival; Cowes Week; Christchurch Regatta; Poole Yachting Week; Cowes/Torquay Power Boat Race; Portsmouth Navy Days; Weymouth Carnival. Sept., Farnborough International Air Show (every two years – '86, '88, etc); Romsey Agricultural and Horse Show; Southampton International Boat Show; Winchester Carnival.

Aldershot   B20
Hampshire (pop. 33,750) Aldershot has long-standing Royal Army associations, and military enthusiasts will enjoy one of the Army's finest museums, the Airborne

Forces Exhibition in Browning Barracks. Among items on display are equipment, medal collections, captured enemy weapons. At Buller Barracks, the Royal Corps of Transport Museum contains uniforms and badges of the Royal Army Service Corps, along with models and photographs of vehicles used from 1795 to today.

The novelist **Jane Austen** wrote the novels *Emma, Mansfield Park* and *Persuasion* while she lived at Chawton House, 22km/14mi SW; it now contains her personal relics. Nearby, **Selborne** was the home of the Rev. Gilbert White, the pioneer naturalist. The Oates Memorial Library and Museum and the Gilbert White Museum contain some galleries devoted to the natural history of Selborne, while others deal with Captain Oates from the famous Antarctica expedition and Frank Oates, one of the explorers of Central Africa.

Bournemouth   H13
Dorset (pop. 153,869) The two Victorian piers are evidence that Bournemouth owed its development to the 19th-century

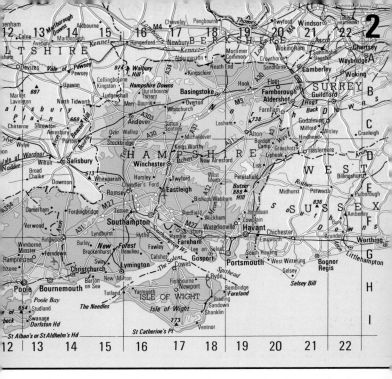

expansion of the seaside holiday industry. Splendid sands, a mild climate and parks and gardens covering one-sixth of the town's area account for Bournemouth's popularity, while 30m/100ft high cliffs add to the town's charm. As well as sports facilities, there are the arts: paintings, china and furniture are displayed in the Rothesay Museum, while Oriental Art is one of the features of the Russell-Cotes Museum. **Poole**, 8km/5mi W, is famous for its Pottery, founded in 1873, and in production ever since.

Christchurch, 8km/5mi E, is dominated by Christchurch Priory, originally part of an old monastery. The church was started in the 11th century and became an Augustinian Priory around 1150. The priory buildings were later destroyed, but the church was retained to serve the parish. 'Tucktonia', in Stour Road, illustrates Britain in miniature, with monuments, pageantry and industrial life shown in a model landscape.

port. Focal points are the High Street and quayside, and it's a popular yachting centre as well as a good base for trips into the New Forest. Buckland Rings, 1½km/1mi N, is an Iron-Age earthwork.

One of the world's finest motor museums is at **Beaulieu**, 10km/6mi NE. It was founded in 1952 by Lord Montagu of Beaulieu in memory of his father, the 2nd Lord Montagu, a pioneer motorist, and contains over 300 veteran and vintage cars, motorcycles, bicycles, commercial and military vehicles. Beaulieu Abbey was founded in 1204 and destroyed by Henry VIII; its refectory is now the parish church. Palace House, once the Abbey gatehouse, was greatly altered in 1870.

Less commercialized is **Buckler's Hard**, 8km/5mi NE, which was a busy shipbuilding centre in the 18th century, turning out among others Lord Nelson's favourite ship *Agamemnon*. The Maritime Museum shows how warships were built from New Forest oak.

Lymington   G15
Hampshire (pop. 35,733) The New Forest meets the sea at this delightful old

Lyndhurst   F15
Hampshire (pop. 2948) Lyndhurst is the 'capital' of the New Forest. The town is

surrounded by attractive woodland scenery with charming, half-wild New Forest ponies wandering freely round the outskirts. See the impressive beech trees in Mark Ash Wood: the Knightwood Oak is about 600 years old, with a girth of over 6m/21ft. The Verderers' Court sits in 17th-century Queen's House on the first or second Monday in January, March, May, July, September and November to administer the forest laws. Other centres with accommodation handy for the New Forest are Brockenhurst, Burley, New Milton, Ringwood, Sway.

Portsmouth G19

Hampshire (pop. 197,431). This old seaport embodies much of Britain's maritime heritage. The old part is near the Round Tower (built 1417), an ancient military fortification. The Square Tower was added later by Henry VII. The Cathedral was originally founded as a church in the 12th century in honour of St Thomas à Becket.

The Naval Base is now a centre of maritime history. Near to HMS *Victory*, Lord Nelson's flagship at the Battle of Trafalgar (1805), are the 15th-century remains of Henry's favourite ship, the *Mary Rose*. Artefacts recovered from the ship are on show in the Mary Rose Exhibition Hall, while the Royal Naval Museum details the great story of the Royal Navy.

Victorian statesman, Lord Palmerston, had Fort Widley built in the 1860s as a counter-measure to the threat of French invasion; (it commands fine views and contains a maze of subterranean passages). The Victorian novelist, Charles Dickens, was born in Commercial Road; mementos of his life are displayed in his house in a reconstructed period setting.

The seaside resort of Southsea merges with Portsmouth on the east side. Southsea Castle, a fort built by Henry VIII in 1539, contains displays of naval and military interest, close to more recent reminders of war in the D-Day Museum. A chronological history of the Royal Marines can be seen in the Royal Marines Museum, Southsea.

Southampton F16

Hampshire (pop. 215,118) Much of Southampton's past revolved around the sea, the source of continuing prosperity since the Middle Ages. Armies left the port for the Crusades and Napoleonic wars and it was from here that the **Pilgrim Fathers** left for America in 1620.

Harbour cruises enable visitors to see the elegant liners and graceful yachts in Southampton Water from the water-line. The old city walls still circle the town in places, and Bargate is one of the finest

town gates surviving; its upper floor contains a museum of local interest. The 14th-century Wool House is now the Maritime Museum. Other museums to visit are in 16th-century Tudor House and Southampton Hall of Aviation. Free guided walks around the medieval town take place daily in summer and on Sundays in winter. Collections of paintings in the Art Gallery include French Impressionists, European Old Masters and 18th–20th-century English works.

Isle of Wight H16

(pop. 109,512) Six km/4mi off the Hampshire shore, the Isle of Wight can be reached by car and passenger ferries – ship, hovercraft and hydrofoil – from Portsmouth, Southsea, Southampton and Lymington. (See p. 15 for details.)

'The Island', as residents call it, was the Roman territory, Vectis, in AD 43; it also had its later share of invasion – by Saxons, Danes and Normans. After the last upheaval, in 1377, when the French burned Yarmouth, Newport and Newtown, it drowsed away, occupied with farming, fishing, smuggling and shipbuilding until the arrival of Queen Victoria at Osborne House (open to visitors), near Cowes, and the advent of the Victorian seaside holiday boom.

Set against a background of hydrangeas, subtropical plants and white cliffs, the resorts of **Sandown**, **Shanklin** and **Ventnor** are grouped on the sheltered south-eastern coast. Away from the pier and seaside amusements, the old part of Shanklin is particularly picturesque with thatched cottages in hollyhock gardens and the Chine – a steep wooded ravine open to visitors. Exotic shrubs bloom outdoors in Ventnor's Botanic Garden, while indoor pleasures include the Museum of Smuggling. **Bonchurch**, 3km/2mi E, has literary associations with eminent Victorians: Swinburne (born and buried here), Thackeray and Macauley (holidayed here), Charles Dickens (wrote here); Tennyson, however, is associated more with **Freshwater** on the Island's west side.

The chalk pinnacles of **The Needles**, 400m/¼mi offshore, mark the Island's western edge. Each rock is individually named – look out for 'Old Pepper', 'Wedge' and 'Frenchman's Cellar'. The south-western coast is notable for its natural beauty: the multi-coloured sands of Alum Bay's cliffs and the 120m/400ft blue clay gorge of Blackgang Chine.

Boat-building began at **Cowes** in the 12th century, and it became a yachting centre six centuries later, made fashionable by the Prince Regent (later George

HMS Victory, *Portsmouth*

IV). There are now nine yacht clubs; the Royal Yacht Squadron is the classiest. Racing takes place between April and Sept., the high spot being Cowes Week in early August.

Yarmouth, with its animated harbour and Tudor castle, lies 16km/10mi W of Cowes, while to the east is **Ryde** with its 800m/½mi long pier. The Island's capital and main harbour, at the head of the tidal estuary of the River Medina, is **Newport**, with a Roman villa which retains several mosaic floors. This little town became the 'new port' in 1180 when Lord of the Island, Richard de Redvers, ruled from nearby Carisbrooke. Carisbrooke Castle (12th-century) had one very important prisoner in 1647–8 – Charles I.

Unspoiled stretches of downs and farmland enhanced by pretty villages make up the inland area. Places to list on your itinerary might include: Haseley Manor and pottery at Arreton; Lilliput Museum of Dolls and Osborn-Smith's Wax Museum, both at Brading and nearby, the fine house, Nunwell Park.

Winchester D16

Hampshire (pop. 35,578) The Anglo-Saxons made Winchester their capital but it had also been important in Roman times. Winchester Cathedral (built 1079–1404) shows the development of architectural styles from massive Norman to graceful Perpendicular. It is the second longest medieval church in Europe and contains the 12th-century Winchester Bible and a Norman font.

Founded in 1136, the Hospital of St Cross is Britain's oldest charitable institution still functioning. Little remains of the Norman castle, but near Westgate is the Great Hall (1235) in which hangs an early fake Round Table of the legendary King Arthur. Medieval Westgate, one of the original five city gates, houses a local history museum.

Other places of interest include: Winchester College, one of England's oldest public schools, founded by William of Wykeham in 1382; Winchester City Museum; the Heritage Centre; Royal Green Jackets Regimental Museum;

Serle's House, an 18th-century house incorporating the Royal Hampshire Regimental Museum; and Wolvesey Castle, remains of a 12th-century bishop's castle.

Channel Islands   B6/H6

The Channel Islands lie off the French coast, over 128km/80mi from southern England. Although part of the British Isles, they do not belong to the United Kingdom, having an independent government with its own laws and taxes.

Jersey, Guernsey, Alderney, Sark and Herm are the main islands; others exist but are not open to visitors. This is Britain's warmest area, with an average temperature of 11°C (52°F) and over 15°C (60°F) from April to October. Getting there is easy by ship, hydrofoil or aircraft (see p. 15), while local boats brave ferocious tides between the major islands.

Jersey, the largest island, is 116sq km/45sq mi. The main town, St Helier, has a population of 35,000; it's a charming place with sleepy squares overlooked by two fortifications – Elizabethan Castle and the Napoleonic Fort Regent (now a leisure centre). Luxury goods are good buys due to tax laws; typical purchases are heavy-knit sweaters and pottery. Places to visit include Gerald Durrell's Zoo at Les Augres Manor; La Mare Vineyards near St Mary; Mont Orgueil Castle, Gorey; Battle of Flowers Museum, St Ouen, and more museums at St Helier and Grouville; the German Underground Hospital, St Lawrence – a reminder of Nazi occupation during World War II.

Guernsey lies 42km/26mi N of Jersey; the journey between islands takes two hours by steamer or 15 minutes by hydrofoil or air-taxi. It comprises 62sq km/24sq mi with a population of 53,000, whose main occupations are tourism and agriculture. The capital, St Peter Port, dominated by Castle Cornet, looks much like a French fishing port. Places to visit in the town include the medieval parish church; Guernsey Museum and Art Gallery; Hauteville House, home in exile of French writer, Victor Hugo; the Royal Court housing Guernsey's island parliament. Frequent buses run to the main beaches: Fermain Bay to the south east; Moulin Huet and Petit Bôt to the south. You might also visit Sausmarez Manor, St Martin's; Guernsey Pottery near St Sampson; Fort Grey Maritime Museum, Rocquaine Bay; German Occupation Museum, The Forest; Underground Military Hospital, St Andrew.

The smaller islands offer attractive walks and beaches but little in the way of organized entertainment. Each island has some hotel and guest house accommodation, but it's best to book ahead. **Alderney** is a peaceful resort island, boasting an airport and one main town, St Anne. Cars are banned from **Sark** and **Herm**; you travel by bicycle or horse-drawn carriage. Anyone seeking solitude and beauty will be well rewarded here.

Mont Orgueil Castle, Gorey, Channel Isles

THE WEST COUNTRY

The West Country is a focal point for British holidaymakers, but you can avoid the crowds by coming in spring or autumn. In any case, plenty of places off the beaten track are well worth visiting.

Dorset is Thomas Hardy country, so if you've read any of his works (*Far from the Madding Crowd*, *The Mayor of Caster-bridge*), you will be familiar with its rural nature. The town of Dorchester masquer-ades as Hardy's 'Casterbridge', while Shaftesbury is 'Shaston'.

Relics of earliest times are scattered throughout the counties of Wiltshire and Avon. Silbury Hill, in Wiltshire, is Europe's largest prehistoric mound, its original purpose still a riddle, while Avebury's stone circle predates ancient Stonehenge (thought to have had religious and astronomical purposes). To get far away from 'sights', you have only to step into the massive beech avenues in Saver-nake Forest south east of Marlborough, while lovely villages like Castle Combe and Lacock exert a siren charm. Cleve-don, Portishead and Weston-super-Mare are the main seaside resorts in this part.

Legend is rife throughout the West Country, especially in Somerset: King Alfred reputedly burnt his cakes at Athel-ney, west of Langport, while the village of Cadbury, in the south, may have been King Arthur's 'Camelot'. With so much romance around, it's hardly surprising that R.D. Blackmore set his novel *Lorna Doone* among the heaths and moorlands of Exmoor, now a National Park. You can explore the Park from coastal Minehead or Georgian South Molton. Alternatively, head through Somerset's winding lanes and apple orchards passing the county town of Taunton and attractive places like Ilminster, Langport, Somerton and Yeovil and on to the Dorset resorts: ele-gant Weymouth and Lyme Regis, beloved of the novelist, Jane Austen.

Following the coast into Devon, you come to a string of holiday resorts: Seaton and Sidmouth, Dawlish and Teignmouth. Torbay comprises three resorts in one: Torquay with its palm trees, harbour and excellent beaches, Paignton which de-veloped with the Victorian seaside indus-try, and Brixham, a fishing port since medieval times. Further along, the mari-time towns of Dartmouth and Plymouth were starting points for historic voyages. The celebrated Elizabethan, Sir Francis Drake, ranks with Sir Walter Raleigh, Hawkins and Grenville among the great seafaring men of Devon. If the coastal spots hold no attraction for you in them-selves, then use them as a base for trips into the massive open space of Dartmoor National Park, a peaceful wilderness dotted by peaks, prehistoric remains, old tin-mines and wild ponies.

Wild Atlantic breakers explode on fine surfing beaches along Devon's north coast, at Woolacombe, Croyde and West-ward Ho! From Bideford you can take a boat-trip to see puffins on Lundy Island. Barnstaple takes its name from the famous market (staple) held here in the days of wool-trading. The colourful Pannier market is a throwback to those times, with goods for sale displayed in large baskets (panniers). Lace, pottery, handwoven cloth, cream and glassware feature among Devon's specialities.

Bodmin Moor introduces England's westernmost part. Cornwall once had its own language (still reflected in numerous place names), and countless stories abound of giants, smugglers and saints. Inland, Cornwall is green and wooded, a lazy countryside where winding lanes flanked by foxgloves dip suddenly to val-leys gilded with furze. Moorland streams ripple beneath 15th-century bridges (like the one at Wadebridge), while disused mine-stacks, half-ruined reminders of the tin industry, finger the skyline around Camborne and Redruth.

Cornwall's coastline is characterized by tiny harbours, rocky headlands and mag-nificent cliffs. Bude and Newquay are the main north-coast resorts, but delightful spots are found all round the long shore-line: Port Isaac, Padstow with its medieval streets, and unselfconscious places like Mullion, Polruan, opposite Fowey, and Coverack, an ancient smuggling centre in the south.

Cider and Cream Teas Devon's rich

dairy farmlands account for the clotted cream and Cheddar cheese enjoyed in the West Country, while Somerset's apple orchards produce not only delicious cider but apple dumplings too. Sea-fishing off Cornwall influences many menus: mackerel, turbot, sole and crab are all caught locally.

Cakes and buns are also a regional feature: Dorset Knobs (biscuits), Lardy Cakes, Bath Buns and Sally Lunn Buns are all popular, while Bath Oliver biscuits are still made to the recipe of Dr Oliver, the spa's 18th-century physician.

The Cornish pasty has long been an economical meal for the working man. In prosperous times the pastry case contained diced vegetables and meat as well as the original ingredient, potato.

As for local beers, try those from J. Arkell of Swindon, Gibbs Mew of Salisbury whose 'Bishop's Tipple' contains no sugar, Wadworth Brewery of Devizes, Devenish Brewery of Redruth and St Austell Brewery.

Markets are held at Barnstaple, Bideford, Wells, Dorchester, Exeter, Bath, Bristol, Chippenham, Devizes, Marlborough, Salisbury, Penzance, Plymouth and Truro.

Festivals and Events March (last week), Bath Antiques Fair. April (first week), Easter hockey festivals – Weymouth and Torbay; mid-April, Badminton Horse Trials. 2–5 May, Torrington May Fair; May (first week), Helston Furry Dance; mid-May, Devon County Show – Exeter; end May, Bath Festival; Royal Bath and West Show – Shepton Mallet. 5–9 June, Bristol Boat Show; June (first week), Royal Cornwall Show – Wadebridge; end June, Church of England Pilgrimage – Glastonbury. Aug. (first week), International Folklore Festival – Sidmouth; mid-Aug., Mid Somerset Agricultural Show – Shepton Mallet; 24 Aug., Mousehole Furry Dance; end Aug., Plymouth Navy Open Days. 10 Sept., Widecombe Fair. 4 Oct., Mop Fair – Marlborough. 12 Oct., Exeter Carnival Week. 26 Dec., Wincanton Race Meeting; National Hunt Racing – Newton Abbot.

Bath   C23

Avon (pop. 84,670) Bath is England's most complete and best-preserved **Georgian city**. Among its famous buildings is No. 1 Royal Crescent, a stone-built Georgian house restored to its original condition and furnished with 18th-century pieces. The Assembly Rooms, designed around 1771 by John Wood the Younger, architect of many of Bath's buildings, were restored after bomb damage during World War II, and now house the Museum of Costume. The well-preserved Roman baths, with England's only hot water springs, adjoin the 18th-century Pump Room in which the waters can still be taken. Collections of porcelain, majolica, silver and miniatures are shown in the Holburne of Menstrie Museum, itself an 18th-century building.

Other places to visit are sumptuous 15th-century Bath Abbey; Bath Carriage Museum in Circus Mews (built 1759); Beckford's Tower, a folly built in neoclassical style in 1827 for novelist William Beckford. Claverton Manor (built 1820) lies 4km/2½mi SE and houses the **American Museum in Britain**, showing decorative arts of the 17th–19th centuries.

Bristol   C22

Avon (pop. 426,657) This attractive university city has been a thriving commercial port since the 10th century, growing up around its harbours on the River Avon. The famous engineer, **Brunel**, built the world's first iron ship, the SS *Great Britain* (1843), which is moored here for restoration. Brunel also built the graceful Clifton suspension bridge from which there are spectacular views along the Avon Gorge.

Bristol Cathedral was founded as an Augustinian monastery in 1148 and incorporates examples of Norman, Early English, Gothic and Victorian architecture. Other places to see include the Church of St Mary Redcliffe, dating from the 13th century; the City Museum and Art Gallery; the Arnolfini Gallery complex; The Georgian House, containing 18th-century furniture and fittings. The Theatre Royal, one of England's oldest theatres still in operation, was opened in 1766 and retains its original decor; it is the home of the Bristol Old Vic company. A fine viewpoint, Cabot Tower, dates from 1898 and commemorates Cabot's discovery of North America in 1497.

Dorchester   J23

Dorset (pop. 13,736) This bustling county town is featured as 'Casterbridge' in the novels of **Thomas Hardy**, who lived 4km/2½mi NE at Higher Bockhampton. You can see a reconstruction of his study in the Dorset County Museum. Military history is on display at the Dorset Military Museum, while the Dinosaur Museum contains prehistoric relics. The Old Crown Court was the scene of the harsh deportation sentence handed out to the Tolpuddle Martyrs for demanding a wage increase in 1834.

Dorchester is surrounded by ancient history: **Maumbury Rings**, on the south edge of the town, is the site of a Stone-Age

3

A

Tintern Parva
Arvans
Chepstow
Wye

22 23 24 Neilsworth Cirencester Lechlade Abingdon 31
Wotton-under-Edge S. Cerney Thames Dorchester
Dursley 25 26 27 28 29 30 Didcot Benson
Tetbury Highworth A419 Vale of White Horse Shrivenham Wantage
Cricklade Whitehorse Hill 856 Berkshire Downs Chiselden East Ilsley Goring
Malmesbury Purton Woetton Bassett A4 Marlborough Downs Lambourn Chieveley Pangbourne
Swindon BERKS M4

B

head
Patchway
Filton
Mangotsfield
Bristol
AVON
(BRISTOL)

Alveston
Chipping Sodbury
Yateo
Coalpit Heath
Kingswood
Marshfield Corsham
Castle Combe
Chippenham
Calne
Avebury
Marlborough
Kennet
Hungerford
Newbury
Kennet
Aldermaston
Heath End
Kingsclere

C

M5
esbury
Chew Magna
Blagdon
Keynsham
Bath
Bradford on-Avon
Melksham
Devizes Vale of Pewsey
Pewsey
974 Walbury Hill
Hampshire Downs
Basingstoke

WILTSHIRE

D

dge
Mendip Hills
Cheddar
moor
Wells
Chew Stoke
Radstock
Midsomer Norton
Trowbridge
A361
Collingbourne Kingston
Hurstbourne Tarrant
Ludgershall
St. Mary Bourne
Overton
Whitchurch

E

tonbury
Shepton Mallet
Beckington
Frome
Westbury
Market Lavington
697
North Tidworth
Andover
Sutton Scotney
Micheldever
Kings Worthy

Evercreech
Warminster
Salisbury Plain
Chitterne
Shrewton
668
Beacon Hill
Over Wallop
Stockbridge

F

erton
port
Castle Cary
Bruton
944
Mere
Wyle
Wylye
Amesbury
Purton
HAMPSHIRE
New Alresford

G

Ilchester
Sparkford
Wincanton
Gillingham
Vale of Wardour
Nadder
Wilton
Broad Chalke
Salisbury
Downton
513
Whiteparish
Hursley
Chandler's Ford
Romsey
Winchester
Itchen
Twyford
Eastleigh
Bishops Waltham

Yeovil
Henstridge
Stalbridge
Shaftesbury
910
Mere

H

erton
port
Crewkerne
Mistarton
Beaminster
Milborne Port
Sherborne
Yetminster
Cerne Abbas
901
Shillingstone
Sturminster Newton
Blandford Forum
Damerham
Fordingbridge
Totton
Southampton
Southampton W.
Sheffield
M2
Wickham
Salisbury
Hamble
Fareham

DORSET

I

/
Beaminster
North Dorset Downs
Wimborne Minster
Ferndown
Ringwood
Lyndhurst
New Forest
Brockenhurst
Hythe
Fawley
Calshot
Gosport

J

Bridport
A35
Maiden Newton
Winterbourne Abbas
Abbotsbury
Puddletown
Tolpuddle
Bere Regis
Broadstone
Poole
Bournemouth
Poole Bay
654
Christchurch
Barton on Sea
Sway
Milford on Sea
Totland
Lymington
Yarmouth
The Solent
Cowes
Fishbourne
Newport
Brading
Sandown

Hampreston

ISLE OF WIGHT

K

715
Weymouth
Wyke Regis
Fortuneswell
Isle of Portland
Dorchester
Frome
Wareham
West Lulworth
Isle of Purbeck
Studland
Swanage
Durlston Hd
St Alban's or St Aldhelm's Hd
The Needles
Isle of Wight
173
Shanklin
Ventnor
St Catherine's Pt

South Dorset Downs
Chesil Beach
Easton

L

M

ENGLISH

N

CHANNEL

O

P

(Map continued westwards overleaf)

Q

R

22 23 24 25 26 27 28 29 30 31

circle adapted by the Romans as an amphitheatre, while **Maiden Castle**, a fine prehistoric fort, 2km/1¼mi SW, was stormed by these same invaders in AD 43. The old priory village of **Cerne Abbas** lies 13km/8mi NW; a giant prehistoric figure is cut into the hillside nearby.

Exeter   J16
Devon (pop. 95,729) The Romans founded Exeter in AD 50 and encircled it *ca* AD 200 with a red stone wall, traces of which are visible off Paul Street and Southernhay. The most attractive areas are Cathedral Close with its medieval buildings, the Georgian terraces of Southernhay and the quay district, east of the two road bridges, with 19th-century warehouses and 17th-century Customs House.

Exeter Cathedral was established in 1050, but rebuilt 1107–37 and again in the 14th century; it is noted for its Gothic vaulting and 14th-century East Window.

Look out for the fine oak panelling in Tucker's Hall, once used by weavers; the 14th-century guildhall; and St Nicholas' Priory, the remains of a Benedictine priory with a Norman undercroft and 15th-century kitchen. Visit also Rougemont House Museum (local history exhibits) and the extensive boat collection in the Maritime Museum. Within easy reach of Exeter are the popular seaside resorts of Exmouth, Budleigh Salterton, Dawlish and Teignmouth.

Falmouth   P6
Cornwall (pop. 18,041) This old Cornish port and popular yachting centre has a fine natural harbour guarded by Henry VIII's castles of Pendennis and St Mawes. Branching creeks and wooded rivers, like the Fal and Helford, snake inland as far as the market town of **Truro** with its Victorian Gothic Revival cathedral.

Falmouth's greatest days were in the 18th century when grain clippers called, after sailing from Australia. Not surprisingly, the 18th- and 19th-century buildings in the older part of town include the Customs House. Since then, a seaside resort has developed with sailing, fishing and safe bathing from four sandy beaches.

A popular excursion from Falmouth heads south across the Helford river to the Lizard peninsula. **Helston** is the main market centre here, achieving fame principally for its Furry (folk) Dance held each May. The Lizard's local history is covered in Helston's Folk Museum. **Lizard Point** is the most southerly part of mainland England, and caves and rocks of serpentine, the characteristic mineral of the Lizard, can be found around Mullion Cove.

Fowey   N9
Cornwall (pop. 2369) This picturesque Cornish seaport was once a haven for pirates, but is now a popular sailing centre, guarded by ruined St Catherine's Castle, another of Henry VIII's defensive strongholds.

Fowey makes a good touring base: take the ferry to the villages of **Bodinnick** and **Polruan**; further east lie **Polperro**, 13km/8mi E, with its interesting museum of smuggling and the former fishing villages of **East** and **West Looe**, 21km/13mi E, now joined by a bridge to form one holiday town. Looe is famous for shark fishing; fierce exhibits are on show at Looe Aquarium, while the Cornish Museum looks closely at local folklore, fishing and tin-mining.

West of Fowey are several little ports and villages – Par, built originally for the shipment of local copper ore, sandy Carlyon Bay, unspoilt Mevagissey, and Gorran Haven. **St Austell**, 16km/10mi W, is a market town and centre of Cornwall's china clay industry; its Wheal Martyn Museum tells you all about this important mineral.

Launceston   K10
Cornwall (pop. 5300) Once an ancient capital of Cornwall, Launceston is now a pleasant market town. A fine round keep forms part of the 12th–13th-century remains of the castle, once the seat of William the Conqueror's brother.

To the west lie **Jamaica Inn**, popularized by Daphne du Maurier's novel of the same name; **Wesley's Cottage** at Trewint, an 18th-century Methodist shrine with interesting testaments and period furnishings; and **Dozmary Pool**, legendary resting-place of King Arthur's sword. More mementos of King Arthur can be seen at **Tintagel** on Cornwall's rugged north coast; the ruined 13th-century castle was his reputed birthplace.

Launceston is within easy reach of the **Dartmoor National Park**, a wild tract of moorland with an average height of 365m/1200ft. Prehistoric remains, treacherous bogs and heights capped by tors (granite outcrops) typify the area. The prettiest scenery is at the edges, but for the intrepid, ideal centres from which to set out walking or riding are Bovey Tracey, Chagford and Yelverton. The information centre at Two Bridges deals with all aspects of the park.

Marlborough   C28
Wiltshire (pop. 6108) This attractive Georgian town, with its wide main street lined by old buildings, lies on the old coaching route between London and

Becky Falls, Dartmoor

Bath. The famous public school was once a coaching inn; a mound in the grounds marks the spot where King Arthur's wizard, Merlin, is supposedly buried.

Marlborough makes a handy centre for visiting numerous prehistoric relics, especially the stone circle at **Avebury**, 10km/6mi W, older even than Stonehenge. It is thought that the circle related in some way to **Silbury Hill**, a mysterious artificial mound 1½km/1mi S of Avebury. Finds made during excavations at nearby West Kennett Long Barrow are displayed in Avebury's Museum.

Ancient trackways can also be found in Savernake Forest, south east of Marlborough, while the **Wansdyke**, a defensive earthwork from Saxon times, caps the downland ridge between Marlborough and the Vale of Pewsey.

Minehead   E16
Somerset (pop. 7370) Minehead doubles as a popular resort and a base for exploring **Exmoor National Park**, especially by

foot or on horseback. Exmoor is principally a plateau, about 305m/1000ft high, although vales alternate with the rolling hills which rise to 520m/1704ft at Dunkery Beacon. Places to visit around Exmoor include medieval **Dunster** with its Tudor houses, massive 12th-century castle and octagonal 17th-century Yarn Market, once used for the sale of locally woven cloth. To the west, along a coastline of sheer cliffs and wooded ravines, is the resort of **Lynmouth** connected to the hilltop town of **Lynton** by a steep road and water-operated cliff railway. In the eastern part of Exmoor, you might explore delightful villages like Luccombe and Winsford and picturesque **Dulverton**, near which is the ancient stone bridge of Tarr Steps.

Penzance   Q2
Cornwall (pop. 19,415) This spacious port and seaside resort makes an excellent base for exploring mainland England's westernmost tip. In 1595 the town was

burned by Spaniards, so there are few early buildings left. Places of interest include the Museum of Nautical Art, located in an old Cornish trading-house and displaying treasure from sunken wrecks; and the Penzance and District Museum at Penlee House.

From the harbour a sandy beach stretches east to Marazion. At low tide you can cross the causeway linking the village to the semi-island of **St Michael's Mount**, or go by ferry (summer only); the castle contains a 14th-century chapel and armour collection.

From Penzance you could visit the pretty fishing village of **Mousehole** (pronounced 'Mowzl') 5km/3mi S; **Chysauster Ancient Village** 6km/4mi N, inhabited between 1st–3rd centuries AD; and the windswept headland of **Land's End**, 16km/10mi SW. All round this peninsula are tiny coves to explore, fishing villages like Sennen and Lamorna Cove, and the tin-mining towns of St Just and Pendeen. **St Ives**, 16km/10mi NE, is an attractive artists' colony with a fine surfing beach. Regular boat and helicopter services leave Penzance for the Scilly Isles 45km/28mi SW.

Plymouth   N12
Devon (pop. 239,452) Due to its magnificent natural harbour, Plymouth has always been a noted seaport, particularly in Elizabethan times. Many famous voyages set out from here, including those made by Sir Francis Drake, who destroyed the Spanish Armada in 1588, and the 101 **Pilgrim Fathers** who embarked from Mayflower Steps on their voyage to the New World in 1620.

The Barbican, with its old inns and shops, the site of the original town as Drake knew it, converges on the harbour of Sutton Pool. Close by, the 16th-century Elizabethan House contains period furnishings. The Hoe, a great open space with panoramic views of Plymouth Sound, was where Drake reputedly finished his game of bowls before routing the Armada. It is capped by Smeaton's Tower, once part of the lighthouse which stood on the Eddystone Rock between 1759–1882. Nearby is the outstanding Aquarium of the Marine Biological Association. Beautiful gardens surround the Tudor mansion, **Saltram House**, 6km/4mi E; more gardens can be enjoyed at **Cotehele House** near Calstock 22km/14mi NW.

Salisbury   F28
Wiltshire (pop. 35,302) The building of the cathedral was the reason for the founding of Salisbury in 1220. This was the only English cathedral of uniform design in the Middle Ages, and it replaced a Norman cathedral (the ground plan of which is at Old Sarum, 3km/2mi N).

The chief features of Salisbury Cathedral are the beautiful tombs, a very early clock (1386) and a library with one of three originals of the Magna Carta. Cathedral Close, entered through medieval gateways, has notable houses from the 12th century onwards including the Old Deanery, the 17th-century North Canonry and 18th-century Mompesson House with its splendid panelling.

Other interesting buildings include the 15th-century Poultry Cross; 18th-century Malmesbury House, noted for its plasterwork; and Church House, once a 15th-century cloth merchant's home. Salisbury and South Wiltshire Museum has displays relating to the city's history.

Wilton House, 5km/3mi W, is the combined architectural work of Inigo Jones and James Wyatt and contains magnificent collections of paintings, furniture and sculpture. The prehistoric monument of **Stonehenge**, 16km/10mi N, dates from the late Neolithic period and early Bronze Age (*ca* 1250 BC); it is thought to have been built for religious and astronomical purposes.

The Isles of Scilly   I3
Cornwall (pop. 2020) This peaceful cluster of about 100 islands lies 45km/28mi SW of Land's End, but only the five largest are inhabited – St Mary's, St Agnes, St Martin's, Tresco and Bryher. The scenery varies from moorlands to granite headlands with numerous secluded sandy beaches. The mild, temperate climate encourages exotic flowers and palm trees; as a result horticulture competes with tourism as the main industry.

Inter-island communication is well organized; you can easily reach the uninhabited islands, like Samson or St Helens, once a retreat for hermits, now populated only by puffins and seals. Most boat-trips leave from **St Mary's** (the largest island although still only 5km/3mi wide) so this is the obvious place to stay. Booking is essential; the best time to come is April or May (see p. 15).

Hugh Town is St Mary's chief centre. Places to visit here are the Isles of Scilly Museum complete with shipwreck display, nearby Longstone Centre including butterfly house and Bant's Carn Burial Chamber. **Tresco** (1½km/1mi by 3km/2mi) has been leased from the Duchy of Cornwall by the Dorrien-Smith family since 1834. Tresco Abbey Gardens contain subtropical plants which bloom even before Christmas.

Stonehenge, Wiltshire

Land's End, Cornwall

The many Bronze-Age tombs throughout the islands have led to the suggestion that they were once used as a burial place; the waters round about are popular with divers searching for sunken treasure.

Taunton   G19

Somerset (pop. 37,444) The county town of Somerset is a lively commercial centre and market town. Its 8th-century castle, restored by the Normans, was the scene of Judge Jeffreys' brutal 'Bloody Assize' (1685), where those associated with the Monmouth Rebellion were tried – the Rebellion ended at the Battle of Sedgemoor, the last battle fought on English soil. Today the castle contains the Somerset County Museum (archaeology, costumes and ceramics).

The parish church of St Mary and nearby church of St James are noted for their splendid towers. Other interesting buildings include Gray's Almshouses (1635); the Octagon Chapel in Middle Street, opened by Methodist John Wesley in 1776; and a well-preserved medieval Priory Barn – while the oldest telephone in the Post Office Telecommunications Museum dates from 1877.

From Taunton, tour round the lovely wooded Quantock Hills or visit **Tiverton** 22km/14mi SW, with its historic castle founded in 1106 and comprehensive folk museum housed in a restored 19th-century school.

Wells   E22

Somerset (pop. 8604) One of England's smallest and loveliest cathedral cities. The chief glories of the cathedral (built 12th–14th centuries) include the Chapter House, the restored West Front and superb Lady Chapel. The Chain Gate leads to Vicar's Close, a street of 14th-century houses. The moated 13th-century Bishop's Palace is open regularly between April and October while episcopal swans in the moat entertain by ringing the drawbridge bell when hungry!

From Wells you can easily reach **Wookey Hole Caves**, 3km/2mi NW, inhabited from 250 BC to AD 400; the 12th–13th-century ruins of **Glastonbury Abbey**, 8km/5mi SW; and the Mendip Hills to the north. Visit also the 5km/3mi long **Cheddar Gorge**, 11km/7mi NW, containing caverns once inhabited by prehistoric man.

Wells Cathedral, Somerset

WALES

Wales is a vigorously individual part of Britain, a land with its own history, tradition, culture and an ancient language still spoken in many areas.

The M4 motorway directly links London and Cardiff (about 240km/150mi) making Wales easy to reach by road, while high-speed trains complete the journey in less than two hours. There are also scheduled flights to Cardiff airport.

The Welsh attitude to life differs subtly from the English. The Welsh people possess a dominant Celtic heritage which, despite subjection to Roman rule, invasion by Saxons, and conquest by Normans, has always manifested itself in fierce patriotism and cultural independence. Not until Henry VIII passed his Statute of Union (1536) did Wales become joined to England. Even unification did little to deter nonconformity in religion – Wesley's 18th-century Methodist movement took firm root throughout Wales – or to weaken political and social radicalism, sparked off particularly by the oppressions of the Industrial Revolution.

The true genius of the Welsh emerges most strongly in the Arts. Hardly surprising, therefore, that the country spawned poets Dylan Thomas, W.H. Davies, R.S. Thomas, painter Augustus John, composer Vaughan Williams, actor Richard Burton and designer Mary Quant. And Welsh tradition is still alive in annual eisteddfods (festivals of music and arts), the best-known being at Llangollen.

Sportsmen are also in their element, for Wales is a great outdoors place offering ample opportunities for mountaineering, angling, pony trekking, watersports or simply walking and admiring the marvellous views.

The landscape is diversity itself: Snowdon's 1085m/3560ft pinnacle rises abruptly from a coastline only 16km/10mi away. The National Parks of Snowdonia and Brecon Beacons are dramatically scenic playgrounds; just as lovely are the protected Areas of Outstanding Natural Beauty along the coast – Gower Peninsula, Lleyn Peninsula and Isle of Anglesey. Even the seaside resorts offer choice, from bustling Llandudno and Rhyl to peaceful spots on Lleyn Peninsula and the Isle of Anglesey. In the south, Cardiff and Swansea are both excellent touring bases with plenty of city-centre attractions including castles, museums, theatres and art galleries. Cardiff, the capital city, plays host to major events like the Searchlight Tattoo held within the castle grounds every two years, as well as the rugby events for which Wales is celebrated.

Wales is also famous for hundreds of castles, many of which formed part of the English King Edward I's defensive chain, and they are noted for their sophisticated military architecture. Then there are the narrow-gauge steam railways to discover, and traditional crafts such as weaving and pottery, details of which can be obtained from the Wales Tourist Board (address on p. 26).

Rarebit and Laverbread Being a nation deeply rooted in the soil, it's natural that many traditional Welsh dishes, such as Poten Ben Fedi (harvest home supper), come from farming communities. The 1200km/750mi long coastline has given rise to traditional seafood recipes like Swper Scadan (herring supper) and Pennog Picl (pickled herrings). Trout and salmon from Welsh rivers also feature predominantly on menus.

Welsh lamb, Welsh rarebit, the Welsh passion for leeks, and teatime treats – Welsh cakes and Bara Brith (speckled bread) – are well known; less famous are laverbread (made from seaweed) and Cawl Mamgu (broth).

Medieval banquets, accompanied by Welsh harp music and folk singing, are held at the castles of Ruthin, Caldicot (south west of Chepstow), Cardiff, and at Melyn Manor near Neath. Traditional folk evenings with Welsh food and entertainment also take place in several hotels (details from Wales Tourist Board).

Markets at Swansea and Llanelli specialize in local produce, particularly seafood (including laverbread); farm produce is also sold at Cardiff market.

Festivals and Events Early April, Swansea Bach Week. Early May, Aberystwyth Festival; mid-May, St David's Cathedral Bach Festival. Mid-June, Llandaff Festival – Cardiff. July (first week), Llangollen International Musical

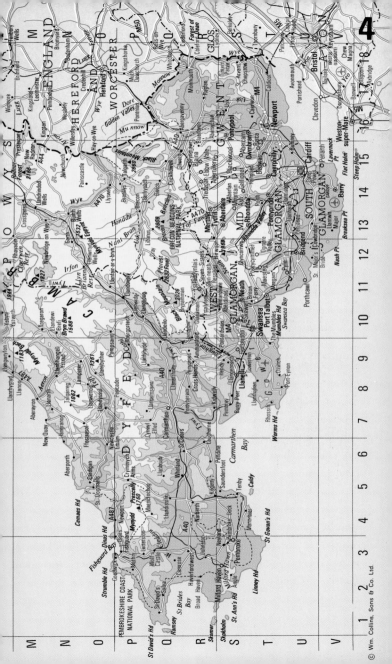

Eisteddfod; late July, Royal Welsh Show – Builth Wells; Gower Festival; Fishguard Festival. Aug. (first week), Royal National Eisteddfod of Wales – venues change annually; Menai Strait Regatta Fortnight. Sept, Victorian Festival – Llandrindod Wells; late Sept., North Wales Music Festival – St Asaph Cathedral. Oct. (first fortnight), Swansea Festival. Late November, Cardiff Festival of Music.

Aberystwyth   K9

Dyfed (pop. 10,688) This seaside resort is also a university town with Theatr y Werin, the university playhouse, which presents a summer season, and an art gallery in the university's Great Hall. The ruined seafront castle dates from the 12th–13th-centuries; more relics – books, prints, deeds – can be found in the National Library of Wales, one of Britain's six copyright libraries.

A favourite with all is the Vale of Rheidol Narrow Gauge Railway, the only steam railway still operated by British Rail, running through beautiful Welsh scenery to Devil's Bridge where the Rivers Mynach and Rheidol meet in a series of spectacular cascades. Details of forest walks can be found in Bwlch Nant-yr-arian Forest Visitor Centre 13km/8mi E, or you might follow the Llywernog Silver Lead Mine Trail 16km/10mi E.

Anglesey, Isle of   B7

From *ca* 150 BC, Anglesey was a centre of Celtic culture and religion, and is particularly renowned for the Druids' long-held stand against their Roman conquerors. Sandy coves, fine beaches and pretty stone-walled villages account for its attraction, along with excellent trout lakes, prehistoric tumuli and cairns, and Edward I's 13th-century **Beaumaris Castle**. Visit the remains of 4th-century **Din Lligwy** Ancient Village off A5025 near Penrhos Llanallgo, and **Bryn Celli Ddu**, a prehistoric burial chamber, 6km/4mi SW of Menai Bridge. Llanfair PG is celebrated for having Britain's longest place name: in full Llanfairpwllgwyngyllgogerychwyrndrobwllllantysyliogogogoch, meaning: St Mary's (church) by the white aspen over the whirlpool and St Tysilio's (church) by the red cave. Main resorts are Moelfre, Benllech, Beaumaris and Holyhead, while inland Llangefni makes a good touring base.

Betws-y-Coed   D10

Gwynedd (pop. 729) Set amid Gwydyr Forest's wooded hills, the village (whose name means Chapel in the Wood) is a good touring centre for Snowdonia. Attractions here include the summer theatre, Theatr Nant y Nos, and Conwy Valley Railway Museum. Nearby beauty spots include Swallow Falls 3km/2mi W of Fairy Glen, and turbulent Conwy Falls 3km/2mi S of Betws-y-Coed.

Dolwyddelan Castle, a restored 12th-century keep, 8km/5mi SW, was the reputed birthplace of Llwelyn the Great. Another locally-born man to create history was **Bishop William Morgan** who first translated the Bible into Welsh; his 16th-century cottage birthplace is off A470, 6km/4mi SW. **Llechwedd Slate Caverns**, 14km/9mi SW, are open to visitors, with more on the slate industry at nearby Gloddfa Ganol.

Brecon Beacons National Park   Q13

Spreading west from Hay-on-Wye and Abergavenny, this 1344sq km/519sq mi National Park is named after the 'Beacons', red sandstone peaks which rise to 885m/2906ft at Pen y Fan; they are thought to have been the site of signal fires.

The National Park Information Centre at Glamorgan St., Brecon, and the Mountain Centre at Libanus will help plan walks and tours, providing details of hikes, geology, flora, fauna. Apart from moorland sheep and wild Welsh ponies, a rich variety of animal, plant and birdlife abounds, while some of the rocks date back 300 million years. Lakes and reservoirs offer sailing, and pony trekking and fishing (salmon, trout, eel) are also popular.

The main centre is the cathedral city of **Brecon**, an excellent town for browsing – in the craft and antique shops, and also round Brecknock Museum (local history) and 24th Regiment Museum (Museum of the South Wales Borderers, a regiment raised in 1689). Another chief centre is the market town of **Abergavenny**, with its ruined 12th-century castle doubling as a local history museum.

Caernarfon   D8

Gwynedd (pop. 9260) Caernarfon's magnificent 13th-century castle, begun by Edward I in 1283 (completed in 1323), was the birthplace of Edward II, first Prince of Wales, and site of the investiture, in 1969, of the present Prince of Wales. It houses the Royal Welch Fusiliers Regiment Museum. At **Segontium**, 1km/½mi E, finds from the Roman military settlement are on display. **Bryn Bras**, 6km/4mi SE, an early Victorian Romanesque castle, has especially beautiful grounds. Caernarfon makes an excellent centre for Snowdonia, Lleyn Peninsula and Anglesey.

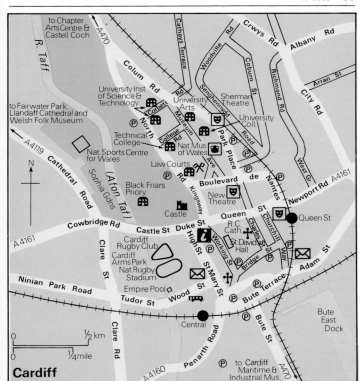

Cardiff

Cardiff U15

South Glamorgan (pop. 279,111) This large seaport, whose prosperity began with the opening of Bute West Dock in 1839, is also the capital of Wales. Cardiff Castle, used by both Romans and Normans, has a 12th-century keep; later additions dating from 1861 include the State Apartments. French Impressionist paintings are given prominence in the National Museum of Wales, behind which is the University College. The Cardiff Industrial and Maritime Museum is located in Bute Town, near the main-road entrance to the docks.

Alongside the River Taff is Cardiff Arms Park National Rugby Stadium and a smaller stadium housing the famous Cardiff Rugby Club. All-year-round sport is enjoyed on Fairwater Park's artificial ski-slope, and for arts-lovers there are the New Theatre, Sherman Theatre and Chapter Arts Centre, while St David's Hall is the National Concert Hall.

Three sights not to be missed are: **Castell Coch**, 8km/5mi NW, a restored 13th-century castle; the interior of **Llandaff Cathedral**, 4km/2½mi NW, reconstructed after war-damage, dominated by Epstein's thought-provoking sculpture *Christ in Majesty*; the open-air **Welsh Folk Museum**, St Fagans, 6km/4mi W, where exhibits, gathered round 16th-century St Fagan's Castle, include a woollen mill, old Welsh farmhouses, a tannery, tollgate and chapel.

Carmarthen Q7

Dyfed (pop. 13,081) The town's Welsh name 'Caerfyrddin', means Merlin's City, and the legendary magician of King Arthur's court was supposedly born here. Carmarthen Castle, once an ancient princely residence, was taken over by the Normans; today only the gateway and towers remain. Although Carmarthen's narrow streets recall earlier periods, the town is predominantly modern and well provided with shops, market (Wed., Sat.) and cattle market (Mon., Wed., Thurs.). Carmarthen County Museum at Abergwili, 3km/2mi NE, contains Neolithic and Stone-Age relics and Roman jewellery.

Ruined 13th-century **Dryslwyn Castle**, 13km/8mi E, played a part in Welsh-English struggles; another native Welsh stronghold is 13th-century **Carreg Cennen Castle**, spectacularly sited, 24km/15mi E. The Swansea-born poet **Dylan Thomas** is buried in Laugharne churchyard 14km/9mi SW; he lived and worked at the Boathouse which is open to visitors.

Conwy   B10

Gwynedd (pop. 12,206) The old heart of this picturesque town is encircled by medieval walls and guarded by a massive 13th-century castle whose walls, 5m/15ft thick, are punctuated with eight drum towers. Contrasting with the castle's bulk is the delicate tracery of Thomas Telford's suspension bridge (1826), on one side of which is Stephenson's tubular bridge (1848) and on the other, the modern road bridge (1958).

From many medieval sights, pick out 14th-century St Mary's Church; Aberconwy, a fine house dating from *ca*1500, now a shop and museum; Plas Mawr, an Elizabethan town house, now housing the Royal Cambrian Academy of Art. Visit also the quayside 'Smallest' House (2m by 3m/6ft by 10ft) furnished as a mid-Victorian Welsh cottage. A good starting point for your walkabout is The Conwy Visitor Centre in Rosehill Street, which provides films and displays and also sells crafts.

Criccieth   F8

Gwynedd (pop. 1505) Criccieth, Pwllheli and the sailing/water-skiing centre of Abersoch are the chief resorts on the Lleyn Peninsula's south shore. Criccieth Castle (13th-century) has a fine gatehouse, while the town itself offers facilities for pony trekking, swimming and fishing (salmon and sea trout).

Lleyn was one of Wales's earliest inhabited parts and, 6km/4mi N of Nefyn, on the lowest of the triple peaks called Yr Eifl (The Rivals) lies Tre'r Ceiri, **Town of the Giants**, an Iron-Age encampment of over 100 hut circles. Another early relic is the holy well, **St Cybi's**, at Llangybi 8km/5mi NW. **Lloyd George Museum** at Llanystumdwy 3km/2mi W contains mementos of the famous Liberal Prime Minister (1863–1945).

Gower Peninsula   T8

The area west of Swansea was Britain's first designated Area of Outstanding Natural Beauty; much of its best scenery is reached on foot. The south and west coasts are rightly recognized for their splendid cliff scenery, sandy coves and surfing beaches; the north has a flatter, marshy coastline. Although coastal attractions predominate, it's pleasant inland too, with plenty to see.

Medieval history abounds in the area: ruined 14th-century **Oystermouth Castle** at The Mumbles; around Oxwich Bay, tumble-down 16th-century **Oxwich Castle** and picturesque 11th-century **Penrice Castle**, neighboured by a late Georgian house (1775) with period plasterwork; **Weobley Castle**, a 12th–14th-century fortified manor house at Llanrhidian.

Harlech   G9

Gwynedd (pop. 1405) Harlech's 13th-century castle is one of Edward I's defensive chain; it's built on the site of an earlier Celtic fortress and has a notable gatehouse. Almost as famous is the 18-hole Royal St David's Golf Club on the dunes! The celebrated song 'Men of Harlech' was composed to commemorate Lancastrian supporter, Dafydd ab Einion, who courageously held the castle during the siege in the 15th-century Wars of the Roses (the first written version dates from the 18th century). Guided tours can be taken round the man-made caverns of Old Llanfair slate quarries.

Llandrindod Wells   M14

Powys (pop. 3460) You can still take the waters in the Pump Room of this Edwardian spa, which attracted 80,000 people annually in its heyday. Llandrindod's fine buildings, spacious parks and comfortable accommodation are legacies of those former days. Golf, angling and boating are popular pastimes and it's also an international bowling venue. Items from the Roman camp at **Castell Collen**, 1km/½mi N, are displayed in the museum. Llandrindod is particularly useful as a base from which to explore and absorb the peaceful beauty of Teme, Lugg and Wye river valleys.

Llandudno   B11

Gwynedd (pop. 19,000) Llandudno, largest of the popular north-coast resorts (the others are Colwyn Bay, Rhyl and Prestatyn), offers the normal seaside day/night-time entertainments. The Great Orme (207m/679ft) offers spectacular

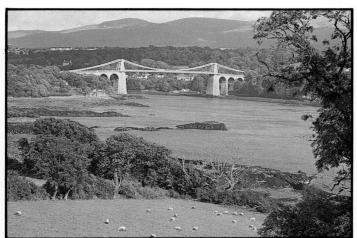

Menai Bridge

Bala Lake, Snowdonia National Park

panoramas of the coastline; its summit is reached by cabin lift or on the Great Orme Tramway, in operation since 1902. Activities might include a tour of Rapallo House Museum, with its old Welsh kitchen and doll collection, or the Mostyn Gallery; a day boat-trip to the Isle of Man; or visits to 19th-century **Bodnant Garden**, 11km/7mi S, and Gilfach, a small shrub garden at **Roewen**, 13km/8mi SW.

Llangollen   E15
Clwyd (pop. 3080) Lying amid typical Welsh scenery, the town is famous for its annual International Musical **Eisteddfod** (folk dancing and singing). Visit Plas Newydd, a timbered mansion with carved oak interior decoration, home of the 'Ladies of Llangollen', 18th-century eccentrics, Lady Eleanor Butler and Miss Sarah Ponsonby. Canal Museum on the Wharf and standard-gauge 'railwayana' in Llangollen Station are also worth a visit.

The River Dee, noted for salmon, is forded by a 14th-century stone bridge, but at **Acrefair**, 3km/2mi NE, the Shropshire Union Canal actually passes above the river, carried by 18th-century Pont-Cysyllte Aqueduct, one of Telford's masterpieces. **Valle Crucis Abbey**, 5km/3mi NW, founded in 1201 for Cistercian monks, has an Early English-style west front; in a nearby field, Eliseg's Pillar is a 9th-century princely memorial. The road climbs to 400m/ 1300ft at Horseshoe Pass, offering views towards Eglwyseg Mountains.

Machynlleth   J10
Powys (pop. 2030) Owen Glendower made Machynlleth the capital of Wales, and the Owain Glyndwr Institute (now the Tourist Information Centre) stands where the famous patriot summoned the last independent Welsh parliament, in 1404. The town is a useful touring centre for the Lower Dovey Valley and the boundary of Snowdonia National Park is only 3km/2mi N across the Dovey bridge. Machynlleth's huge clock tower dates from 1873, while houses in the street named Maen Gwyn date from the 17th–19th centuries.

Menai Bridge   C8
Gwynedd (pop. 2340) The spectacular road bridge, spanning Menai Strait and linking Anglesey with mainland Wales, was built by Thomas Telford in 1825. It is 305m/1000ft long, 30m/100ft above high water and offers marvellous views along the Strait. Nearby is Britannia Railway

Bridge, erected by Stephenson in 1850, burned in 1970, but now restored. Chiefly an angling and yachting centre, the town has an interesting Museum of Childhood and Art Gallery.

Ancient reminders nearby include **Bryn Celli Ddu**, a prehistoric burial place, 6km/4mi SW; **Penmon Dovecote** dating from *ca* 1600, at the Penmon Priory site off B5109 13km/8mi NE; and remains of 4th-century **Din Lligwy** Ancient Village, off A5025 14km/9mi NW.

Pembrokeshire Coast National Park   P1
This National Park follows the south-west coastline for about 240km/150mi, but is rarely over 8km/5mi wide except where the Preseli Hills spread inland. The Park is specially noted for dramatic cliffs lashed by Atlantic breakers, while off-shore islands, like Ramsey and Skomer (both nature reserves), are breeding-grounds for grey seals and seabirds (razor-bills, fulmars, gannets).

Fishguard is the busy port for trips to Ireland, while attractive resorts along St Bride's Bay include Solva, a former smugglers' haunt, Newgale and Marloes. **Milford Haven**, a leading port and oil-refining town, was founded by Sir William Hamilton whose wife, Lady Emma Hamilton, was Nelson's mistress. Creeks snake inland to the lively market town of **Haverfordwest** with its 12th-century castle, now a museum and art gallery. More pictures, chiefly inspired by the Pembrokeshire countryside, are displayed in the Graham Sutherland Gallery, **Picton Castle**, 6km/4mi E. Other places of interest include: one of Britain's most impressive Norman castles at **Pembroke**; near Pembroke, 13th-century **Carew Castle** with nearby 4m/14ft high Carew Cross dating from *ca* 1033 and engraved with Celtic carvings; ruined 13th-century **Lamphey Palace**. **Bosherston's** 5km/3mi lake is gloriously covered with summer water lilies, while St Govan's Head is famous for the tiny 13th-century Chapel of St Govan perched on the cliffside.

Information centres at: St David's, Haverfordwest, Pembroke, Tenby, Fishguard, Broad Haven, Kilgetty.

Porthmadog   F9
Gwynedd (pop. 3840) Porthmadog and its twin town, Tremadog, form the gateway to the Lleyn Peninsula; both towns were built on reclaimed land in the 19th century. Yachting, fishing and touring Snowdonia are popular pastimes. You might also buy

Porthmadog pottery from the Snowdon Street Mill, or visit the Maritime Museum at the harbour where a sailing ketch, *Garlandstone*, houses seafaring displays.

Ffestiniog Narrow Gauge Railway takes you on a scenic journey into the hills. It was opened in 1836 to carry slate from mines at Blaenau Ffestiniog to the sea; the Porthmadog end has a railway museum.

Portmeirion, 3km/2mi SE, is the Italianate dream-village of Sir Clough William-Ellis, and has a range of pottery named after it. At nearby Penrhyndeudraeth, the Saltings Pottery has its own attractive range.

Ruthin D14

Clwyd (pop. 4338) This old market town is an ideal centre for discovering North Wales's lesser-known valleys; its many shops specialize in traditional Welsh fare and local crafts – as at the Ruthin Craft Centre. In the Wars of the Roses Ruthin

was fortified for the Lancastrians and again for the Royalists in the Civil War; a nightly curfew has been rung at 2000 hours since the 11th century.

Ruthin Castle, originally a medieval fortress, then a 19th-century castle, is now a hotel. Other interesting buildings include Plas Coch, rebuilt 1613; 14th-century St Peter's Church; half-timbered Exmewe Hall and the Old Court House (both now Banks); 14th-century Nantclwyd House (exterior only). Maen Huail (Huail's stone) is the block on which King Arthur reputedly had Huail, his rival in love, beheaded.

St David's Q1

Dyfed (pop. 1638) This small village is only a city by virtue of its cathedral, named after St David, patron saint of Wales. The first Bishop-Abbot, St David, died during the 6th century, after which St David's blossomed into a focal point for pilgrimages. The present building, an

Pembroke Castle

excellent example of the transition from Norman to Early English architecture, was erected in 1178 and added to later. Particularly noteworthy are the Irish oak roof in the nave, 35m/116ft tower, and carved misericords in the choir. Music recitals take place July–September. Remains of the 13th-century Bishop's Palace lie nearby.

Snowdonia National Park   F10

An area, 2175sq km/840sq mi, comprising mountains, lakes, forests and 40km/25mi of coastline, makes up this National Park, with helpful Centres at Betws-y-Coed, Llanberis, Aberdovey, Blaenau Ffestiniog, Harlech, Bala and Dolgellau. As well as a playground, this is a working landscape, and sheep farming and forestry are major activities. Fishing is excellent (salmon and trout) and there are nature and forest trails to follow.

Snowdon Mountain Railway climbs Snowdon's 1085m/3560ft peak, while the Snowdon Sherpa, a circular bus service, runs from town centres such as Porthmadog, Beddgelert, Llanrwst, Betws-y-Coed, Caernarfon, and the climbing resorts of Capel Curig and Llanberis.

Swansea   T10

West Glamorgan (pop. 173,413) Wales's second largest city is also a leading port, home of University College and birthplace of poet Dylan Thomas. Rare Swansea porcelain can be admired in Glynn Vivian Art Gallery and Museum; other collections include local finds at the Royal Institution Museum and old vehicles in the nearby Industrial and Maritime Museum. Swansea's excellent shopping facilities include local Welsh fare on sale in Wales's largest market. County cricket and first-class rugby are played on St Helen's Ground; more sport is found in the Leisure Centre with its indoor beach and pool with artificially induced waves, while the city's maritime quarter has been revitalized with a 600-berth marina complex.

Touring prospects are extensive: eleven local castles, including Swansea's 16th-century fortress, plus a ruined Cistercian abbey at **Neath**, 11km/7mi NE. **Port Talbot**, 11km/7mi SE, has one of Europe's largest steelworks.

Tenby   S5

Dyfed (pop. 4994) Places to visit in this old walled town include 13th-century ruined Tenby Castle; Tenby Museum containing interesting geological specimens; gabled 15th-century Tudor Merchant's House, the ground floor of which is now a National Trust Information Centre.

Manorbier Castle, 8km/5mi SW, the birthplace of 12th-century historian Giraldus Cambrensis, retains its original chapel, hall and gatehouse. **Caldey Island**, 5km/3mi offshore and reached by launch, has an ancient priory church and modern monastery where Cistercian monks produce and sell perfume made from wild flowers which are gathered on the island.

Wrexham   E16

Clwyd (pop. 39,052) North Wales's principal industrial centre is also an important market town. The churchyard of 15th-century St Giles's Church, with its brilliant soaring 40m/135ft steeple, contains the tomb of **Elihu Yale**, after whom Yale University in USA is named. **Gresford**, 5km/3mi N, has another fine church boasting a famous peal of twelve bells, while 1½km/1mi S stands **Erddig**, a late 17th-century house (National Trust) containing fine furnishings, with restored outbuildings – laundry, bakehouse, smithy and sawmill.

Wye Valley   S18

The Wye, a noted salmon river, is also famous for the wooded glory of its valley. Medieval walled **Chepstow** has long been a strategic centre, guarded by an 11th–13th-century castle, and its museum displays all aspects of the Wye. Worthwhile excursions from Chepstow include **Caerwent**, 8km/5mi SW, Wales's only Roman civilian town, built AD 75; the Roman amphitheatre at **Caerleon** 19km/12mi SW, and Norman **Caldicot Castle** and Countryside Park, 8km/5mi SW, where medieval banquets take place on weekdays.

North of Chepstow the Wye, passing the Wyndecliffe, a celebrated viewpoint, winds round majestic ruined **Tintern Abbey**, founded by Cistercian monks in 1131, and active until Henry VIII's Dissolution of the Monasteries in the 16th century. Another king – Henry V – was born in the 12th-century castle keep at the historic market town of **Monmouth**, where unexpected features include the museum's collection of Nelson relics and a unique 13th-century fortified bridge gateway. As for Border strongholds, there's plenty of choice: 15th-century **Raglan Castle** 11km/7mi SW; restored 13th-century **Pembridge Castle** 6km/4mi NW; **Skenfrith Castle** 10km/6mi NW; 13th-century **White Castle** 13km/8mi NW.

HEART OF ENGLAND

Little has changed over the centuries in the Cotswolds, where gentle uplands are studded with beautiful old villages and towns, frequently built from the locality's yellow limestone and often graced by magnificent churches erected chiefly from the wealth of the medieval wool trade.

The Rivers Avon and Severn are the two important watery arteries of this heartland, passing through some of England's most famous landscapes. The Severn winds through the ancient city of Worcester, skirting the Malvern Hills to meet the Avon at historic Tewkesbury, a few miles from the Roman fording-point which gave birth to the city of Gloucester.

The Avon flows past a renowned garden valley, the Vale of Evesham, alive with pastel-coloured blossoms in spring and heavy with asparagus, tomatoes and fruit in their seasons. The Avon also passes Stratford, the home of William Shakespeare; and all round Stratford there is the England he loved and reflected in his writings: peaceful villages, half-timbered towns, quiet green countryside.

Another lovely river is the Wye, which passes through Herefordshire's rich red fields and meadows full of cider apples, hops and white-faced red cattle. The hub is Hereford where, every third year since 1727, music-lovers have come to enjoy the Three Choirs Festival. Characteristic black-and-white buildings decorate the villages and are best seen at Ledbury, in the old wool town of Leominster, and in villages like Pembridge, Weobley and Eardisland.

The dark mountains of Wales give way to the area called The Marches and the English hills of Long Mynd, Wenlock Edge and Clun Forest. The expression 'The Marches' comes from an Anglo-Saxon word for boundary – the border with Wales. As the name suggests, the area was once less tranquil than today; its turbulent past is indicated by ancient barrows, pre-Roman camps and Offa's Dyke – an entrenchment which once guarded the ancient kingdom of Mercia (a long-distance footpath runs the entire length). In turn, the Normans left remains of splendid castles at Shrewsbury, Goodrich and the medieval riverside town of Ludlow.

Throughout this western part, the hamlets are often no more than a church and a couple of farms, so be warned – a decent meal is hard to come by outside the larger towns. The charm of the area, however, lies in this very remoteness and diversity: from the hopfields of Tenbury Wells in Worcestershire, and the faded Victorian spa of Church Stretton in Shropshire to steep Bishop's Castle on the approaches to The Marches.

The great hills of the Peak District National Park rise to the north in Staffordshire. Here the bare rocky hills and sturdy stone houses are typical of the Pennines, but give way to the moorland and forest of Cannock Chase – the historic county town of Stafford makes a good base for walking and riding in this former royal hunting ground. The focal point of north Staffordshire is the Five Towns (in reality six) of Arnold Bennett's *Clayhanger* and other novels set in the towns of The Potteries, with their famous china factories of Wedgwood (which has a special visitor centre), Minton, Spode and Royal Doulton.

Beef and Cider Many major breweries are based in the noted brewing centre of Burton upon Trent; further south, Donnington and Whitbread produce their own varieties of beer. Cider comes from Herefordshire's apples while teetotallers can enjoy pure Malvern Water.

Hereford cattle provide excellent beef, while the rich grasslands produce milk for Double Gloucester cheese and, more unusually, Single Gloucester which is available on market stalls in Gloucestershire and Herefordshire. Local rivers offer an abundant supply of salmon for use in dishes like Wye Baked Salmon.

Markets worth visiting include those at Cheltenham, Droitwich, Evesham, (outlet for fruits grown abundantly in the Vale of Evesham), Gloucester, Great Malvern, Hereford, Ross-on-Wye, Stroud and Worcester.

Festivals and Events March, Cheltenham Gold Cup (National Hunt horserace). April to Dec., Shakespeare Festival – Stratford-upon-Avon. May, Malvern Festival of Shaw and Elgar works. June, Three Counties Show – Malvern; Pershore Festival of Music and Art; June/July, Ludlow Festival. July, Royal Show – Stoneleigh; Cheltenham International Festival of Music; Lichfield Festival; Shrewsbury International Music Festival. Aug., Cheltenham Cricket Festival; Shrewsbury Flower Show; Three Choirs Festival – different venues (check with Tourist Information Centre); Town and Country Festival – Stoneleigh. Sept., Bromyard Folk Festival. Oct., Stroud Arts Festival; Cheltenham Literary Festival.

Birmingham H10

West Midlands (pop. 1,014,670) Britain's second largest city and industrial centre boasts excellent shopping facilities and exciting nightlife. The City Museum and Art Gallery has a fine array of Pre-Raphaelite (19th-century) paintings, while the Museum of Science and Industry houses the earliest English locomotive (built 1784) among its vast collection of 19th-century mechanical apparatus. Also worth visiting are the Botanical Gardens to the south west at Edgbaston, laid out in 1831 by Loudon; the fine Jacobean mansion of **Aston Hall**, 5km/3mi N, now a museum; and **Blakesley Hall** at Yardley, 10km/6mi SE, a timber-framed partly furnished yeoman's farmhouse (built ca1600). **Packwood House**, 19km/12mi SE, is famous for its remarkable mid-17th-century yew garden representing Christ's Sermon on the Mount.

Burton upon Trent E11

Staffordshire (pop. 50,201) The air of this pleasant town is pervaded with the scent of hops and malt, for Burton has been famous as a brewing centre since the Middle Ages and has a fascinating Brewing Museum. Although most beer today is produced in huge vats, Bass beer is still brewed in individual barrels as it has been since the 18th century. Michael Bass (later Lord Burton) gave the town some of its finest Victorian buildings, including the town hall and St Paul's Church.

Cheltenham O9

Gloucestershire (pop. 74,356) A legacy of Regency period architecture has been inherited from the days when Cheltenham was a fashionable spa. Spa water can still be taken at the Pittville Pump Room, Cheltenham's most beautiful building. The **Gustav Holst Museum** is con-

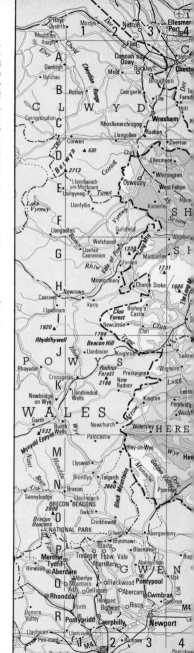

tained within the house where this famous composer was born.

Cheltenham is a lively centre for music, art and sport, with a Music Festival in July and a Festival of Literature in October. Racing and cricket are predominant sports, and the Cheltenham Gold Cup Meeting (March) is one of the main features in the English racing calendar.

Cirencester   Q10

Gloucestershire (pop. 11,990) Three Roman roads – Akeman Street, the Fosse Way and one of the two Ermine Streets – radiate from Cirencester, which was the largest Roman town after London in the 2nd century AD. Many exciting Roman finds, including coins and mosaics, are housed in the Corinium Museum, while remains of a Roman amphitheatre stud Quern Hill. By the 15th century, Cirencester was England's greatest wool market and it was during this period that the Church of St John the Baptist was built; it contains fine brasses of medieval wool and wine merchants.

Cirencester is a good centre for touring **Cotswold villages** like Bibury, 11km/7mi NE, and Bourton-on-the-Water, 24km/15mi NE. You might also visit **Chedworth Roman Villa**, at Yanworth 13km/8mi NE; and **Westonbirt Arboretum** near Tetbury 21km/13mi SW, a splendid example of a 19th-century arboretum.

Coventry   I13

West Midlands (pop. 335,238) Although Coventry's history dates back to the 8th century, it was badly bombed in World War II and almost entirely rebuilt. Alongside the blackened ruins of the old cathedral, an outstanding new cathedral, designed by Sir Basil Spence, was consecrated in 1962. Inside, Graham Sutherland's tapestry of 'Christ in Glory', said to be the world's largest, dominates the nave. The Cathedral Visitor Centre reveals the chequered history of the town and cathedral. Among Coventry's few remaining medieval buildings is St Mary's Hall, formerly a merchants' guildhall. A statue in Broadgate Street commemorates Lady Godiva who reputedly rode naked through the streets in 1043 in a game bid to persuade her husband, Leofric, Earl of Chester, to reduce the townspeople's taxes.

Rugby, 19km/12mi SE, is synonymous with the famous public school of the same name (founded 1567), the scene of Thomas Hughes' novel *Tom Brown's Schooldays*, and where, in 1823, the game of rugby football is said to have originated.

Evesham   M10

Hereford and Worcester (pop. 13,855) This old town is a market centre for the Vale of Evesham – come in springtime and see the glorious blossom! The Almonry Museum, a 14th-century stone and half-timbered building, exhibits the culture and history of the Vale since prehistoric times. The town is a good centre for exploring **Cotswold villages** like Broadway 8km/5mi SE, Buckland 11km/7mi SE and Chipping Campden 13km/8mi SE.

Gloucester   O8

Gloucestershire (pop. 90,232) Gloucester's origins date back to pre-Roman times, but the magnificent cathedral was begun later, in the Norman period. It was partially transformed by Edward III's masons who originated the Perpendicular style (copied throughout the country) in order to turn the Norman choir into a resting-place for Edward II's tomb; the fan-vaulting in the cloisters was an innovation in its day. At the Brass Rubbing Centre you can take rubbings from replica brasses during the summer. Bishop Hooper's Lodging contains a folk museum housed in the half-timbered building associated with this 16th-century Protestant martyr. The 19th-century docks are also worth visiting.

Great Malvern   M7

Hereford and Worcester (pop. 29,000) This spa town is set in the 14km/9mi range of the Malvern Hills; its modern history possibly owes its origins to a treatise by Dr Wall, published in 1756, extolling the medicinal virtues of the waters of Malvern Well. The Norman Priory Church of Saints Mary and Michael is Malvern's most cherished possession. It was built *ca*1086, but reconstructed in the 15th century, and has marvellous medieval stained glass and misericords.

Tewkesbury, 13km/8mi SE, is a classic example of a half-timbered English town with a maze of medieval alleyways and interesting old inns.

Hereford   M4

Hereford and Worcester (pop. 46,503) Hereford is a peaceful country town whose cathedral dates from the 12th century; treasures include the internationally renowned *Mappa Mundi, ca* 1290, a typical medieval map. St John & Coningsby Museum displays armour and costumes and contains the Dining Hall and Chapel (*ca* 1170) of the Knights of St John. The Museum of Cider is open April–October.

Hereford was once the Saxon capital of the kingdom of West Mercia. Today it is a

Priory Church, Great Malvern

good centre for visiting **Offa's Dyke**, a 224km/140mi wall and ditch built in the 8th century by Offa, Saxon King of Mercia. The dyke divided England from Wales and ran from Chepstow to Cheshire; there's still evidence of it at Kington and Clun.

Ironbridge G6

Shropshire It was here that, in 1709, Abraham Darby first smelted iron using coke instead of charcoal, making the technological breakthrough which triggered off the Industrial Revolution. A series of museum sites display unique monuments to the industrial past: the world's first iron bridge, designed by Abraham Darby; Blists Hill open-air museum with a working saw mill, tollhouse and inclined canal; Coalbrookdale Museum, the site of the original furnaces; Coalport China Works Museum. Ironbridge is set in an attractive wooded gorge.

Lichfield G11

Staffordshire (pop. 22,660) Despite rapid modernization, Lichfield retains much of its former charm. The city is dominated by the cathedral's three graceful sandstone spires, known as 'the Ladies of the Vale'. The present cathedral dates from the 14th century; its treasures include 16th-century stained-glass windows in the Lady Chapel and, in the cathedral library, *St Chad's Gospels*, one of Europe's finest illuminated manuscripts. The 18th-century writer **Samuel Johnson** was born, in 1709, in a house on Breadmarket Street (now a Johnsonian Museum). In the cobbled square stands a statue of Dr Johnson and opposite, a monument to his biographer, James Boswell. The Norman keep and tower of **Tamworth Castle** lie 11km/7mi SE.

Ludlow J5

Shropshire (pop. 6780) Delightful half-timbered buildings give a medieval air to this attractive town. The massive red sandstone castle was built in 1085; Shakespearian plays are performed in the castle bailey during the annual summer festival.

The graceful interior of the Church of St Lawrence (Ludlow's patron saint) mainly dates from the early 15th century. **Stokesay Castle**, 10km/6mi NW, is one of England's finest 13th-century fortified manor houses. The **Acton Scott Working Farm Museum**, 18km/11mi N, demonstrates agricultural practice as it was at the turn of the century, prior to the advent of electricity.

Nuneaton   H13

Warwickshire (pop. 67,027) Nuneaton is closely associated with the 19th-century writer **George Eliot** – the pen-name of Mary Ann Evans – whose books include *Middlemarch* and *The Mill on the Floss*. Nuneaton Library has first editions of her books, manuscripts and letters; and the Museum houses a George Eliot Collection. Arbury Hall, a unique Elizabethan and 18th-century Gothic house, was featured as 'Cheverel Manor' in her novel *Mr Gilfil's Love Story*. Other George Eliot associations can be found in Astley, Chilvers Coton and Coventry (details from Tourist Information Centre).

Ross-on-Wye   O6

Hereford and Worcester (pop. 6390) The origins of this peaceful market town may go back to Roman times, but its essential character is due to one benefactor, John Kyrle, in the late 17th century. Among many examples of his town planning is the Prospect, a walled public garden near the 14th-century church. Kyrle's house was at 34 Market Place; 'Kyrle's Walk' starts from a stone arch at the south-west side of the Prospect. Places to visit nearby include ruined **Goodrich Castle** 6km/4mi S and an interesting **Falconry Centre** with demonstrations and museum at Newent, 13km/8mi E.

Shrewsbury   F5

Shropshire (pop. 56,188) Everywhere you go in this county town (pronounced 'Shrosebry'), you'll see superb black-and-white buildings in plaster and weathered timber, including Abbot's House (1450); tall gabled Ireland's Mansion (1575) and early 16th-century Rowley's House, which has a museum of Roman remains from the excavations at Wroxeter. The castle ruins date from the time of Henry II. It was enlarged by Edward I, and in 1790 it was saved from disrepair by the famous engineer, Thomas Telford; it now contains a military museum.

A 16km/10mi ridge of hills called **The Long Mynd** lie 16km/10mi S, and provide some of Shropshire's finest walking country where the remains of prehistoric earthworks crown hilltops.

Stoke-on-Trent   C8

Staffordshire (pop. 265,258) Stoke is the largest of six separate towns which comprise Stoke-on-Trent; the others are Longton, Fenton, Hanley, Burslem and Tunstall. This is the heart of the area known affectionately as 'The Potteries', (depicted so clearly in the novels of 19th-century writer **Arnold Bennett**), where England's famous clayware is made. You can see a working pottery with original machinery and bottle-ovens in the Gladstone Pottery Museum at **Longton** 3km/2mi SE, while the Wedgwood Visitor Centre at **Barlaston**, 8km/5mi S, lets visitors talk to skilled craftsmen. **Trentham Gardens** on the south-east edge of Stoke is a 280-hectare/700-acre estate renowned for its Italian Gardens. Or you may enjoy the questionable pleasure of descending 213m/700ft into a coalmine at the Chatterley Whitfield Mining Museum, **Tunstall**, 5km/3mi NW.

Stratford-upon-Avon   L11

Warwickshire (pop. 19,452) This old market town was the birthplace of 16th-century playwright and poet, **William Shakespeare**, on 23 April 1564. The World of Shakespeare multi-media presentation takes you back to the England of 1575 and among many buildings associated with the poet is the reputed (and likely) birthplace in Henley Street – a half-timbered house containing numerous relics. There are also Hall's Croft, a Tudor house and former home of Shakespeare's daughter, Susanna; Anne Hathaway's

Mary Arden's house, Wilmcote

Warwick Castle

Cottage at Shottery, a village 1½km/1mi W; and Mary Arden's house at Wilmcote, 6km/4mi NW, the Tudor birthplace of Shakespeare's mother. Holy Trinity Church, beautifully situated by the River Avon, contains the poet's grave.

Stratford also contains many other 15th- and 16th-century timber-framed houses and interesting 18th-century buildings. **Harvard House** (built 1596) was the home of the mother of John Harvard, who founded Harvard University in the USA. Cars are displayed in period settings in **Stratford Motor Museum**, while at the **Brass Rubbing Centre** you can make rubbings (materials provided) from replicas moulded from original brasses in English churches.

Charlcote Park, 5km/3mi NE, is a restored Elizabethan house where Shakespeare was reputedly brought before the owner, Sir Thomas Lucy, for poaching in the deer park. **Ragley Hall**, 13km/8mi W, 17th-century home of the Seymours, contains fine porcelain and furniture.

Hotels in Stratford get very busy April–Nov., so be sure to book ahead.

Warwick   K12

Warwickshire (pop. 18,296) Warwick's crowning glory is its 14th-century castle which contains a magnificent collection of paintings by Rubens, Van Dyck and Reynolds. Caesar's Tower, rising nearly 45m/150ft above the River Avon was built in 1370; Guy's Tower was added in 1394. On regular 'medieval' afternoons you can see the castle knights and medieval singers and dancers. Warwick has a fine collection of half-timbered buildings including Lord Leycester's Hospital, built in 1383 originally as a guildhall and converted to a hospital in 1571.

Royal Leamington Spa, 5km/3mi NE, owes its popularity to the medicinal springs which were known in the 16th century and became famous in the 18th century. Today the waters are still used for the treatment of physical ailments; mental relief is provided by Warwick Art Gallery, where British and Dutch paintings are a speciality.

At **Kenilworth**, 8km/5mi N, Norman barons again successfully adapted a Saxon site when they built their castle. Its keep dates from 1155–70, with a great hall added in the 14th century by John of Gaunt, powerful Duke of Lancaster.

Worcester   L8

Hereford and Worcester (pop. 73,452) This ancient city is dominated by its magnificent cathedral, dating from 1084. Other notable buildings include the restored 18th-century guild-hall; Tudor House, a 500-year-old timber-framed house now a museum of local life; and The Commandery, a 15th-century hospital, now housing local history displays. The Dyson Perrins Museum contains the world's finest collection of Worcester china. The cottage at Lower Broadheath, 5km/3mi W, where Sir **Edward Elgar** was born in 1857, is now a small museum.

THAMES & CHILTERNS

The source of the Thames is said to be a spring near the village of Coates in Gloucestershire; even if this is so, the river is merely a trickle for many miles. As it flows through Oxfordshire, it is swelled by four main tributaries: the Windrush Evenlode, Cherwell and Thame. Between Lechlade and Oxford, it's all grassy meadows, willow trees, locks and boats. At any moment you expect to find Ratty and Mole (from the children's classic, *The Wind in the Willows*, written by Kenneth Grahame at Pangbourne, in Berkshire) sunning themselves on the banks.

To the west are the Oxfordshire Cotswolds – gently rolling hills sheltering peaceful villages, built of local honey-coloured stone, and historic towns. South of Oxford's dreaming spires, each town has its own place in time: Dorchester, once an important Roman settlement; Thame with its market and old inns; Faringdon, whose history predates the Norman Conquest. And from ancient Abingdon to Wallingford, soundless loops of river wind their way to the busy boating waters of the Lower Thames.

More hills close to the Thames are the gentle Berkshire Downs, with centres like Wantage (King Alfred's birthplace) and Newbury, where strings of racehorses go gracefully to morning exercise along chalk uplands. The Downs are crisscrossed by ancient byways like the Roman Icknield Way and prehistoric Ridgeway.

Footpaths are also a feature of the wooded Chiltern Hills which run through Buckinghamshire and Bedfordshire before fading out in Hertfordshire and Cambridgeshire. The hills provide vantage points at Coombe Hill (over 260m/850ft) near Wendover and Ivinghoe Beacon (about 250m/811ft) north of Tring, and are particularly fine in autumn when the leafy beech trees turn to red-brown.

Buckinghamshire has been a centre of civilization since prehistoric times and has nurtured its share of famous people: William Cowper wrote most of his poems at Olney; Thomas Gray was inspired to compose his famous *Elegy* in Stoke Poges churchyard; while William Penn, the Quaker founder of Pennsylvania, USA, came from the village of Penn, north east of High Wycombe.

Apart from stretches of the Chilterns, Hertfordshire is mainly a gentle countryside. Its intimate charm was a considerable attraction for the Romans, who made one of their largest English towns at St Albans. Hertfordshire was also favoured by the writers Charles Lamb and George Bernard Shaw, while further literary links can be picked up in Bedfordshire where there is evidence of the religious writer John Bunyan's associations with Bedford.

Puddings and Jam Many local recipes come from Oxford's colleges, proving that their hospitality matches the fineness of their intellectual pursuits. New College Pudding, a fried suet pudding with currants and peel, dates from the 19th century; Oxford Pudding is savoury and filled with pork, liver, bacon, onion, chestnuts and veal. Oxford Jam (sliced meat in a lemon sauce) and Oxford marmalade are also associated with the county.

Puddings are popular in this area – try Bacon Badger, Bacon Pudding and Windsor Bean Pudding. Other traditional fare includes Aylesbury Duck, Brown Windsor Soup and Banbury Cakes.

Flourishing local breweries producing noted beers include Morrells in Oxford, who brew a high-gravity barley wine called College Ale; Morlands in Abingdon (Britain's oldest independent Brewery); and Brakspear's based in Henley.

Markets selling fresh produce are held at Oxford, Banbury, Wallingford and Thame, while locally made foods, such as jams, are on sale at Abingdon and Witney.

Festivals and Events Shrove Tuesday, Olney Pancake Race. 1 May, May morning Celebrations – Magdalen College, Oxford; early May, Morris Dance Festival – Bampton; Royal Windsor Horse Show; Annual Street Fair, Bampton; Live Crafts Festival Exhibition – Hatfield House; Ascension Day, Beating of the Bounds – Oxford; end May, Bedford River Festival. Mid-June, Reading Regatta; Marlow Regatta; Royal Ascot; end June, Mayor of Ock Street election (morris dancing festival) – Abingdon. Early July, Henley Regatta; mid-July, Bedford Regatta; Rose Festival – St Albans. Early Sept., Buckinghamshire County Show – Aylesbury; mid-Sept., Thame Agricultural Show. 11 Nov., Firing of Poppers (miniature cannons) – Fenny Stratford. 26 Dec., Annual Meet of Heythrop Hunt – Chipping Norton.

Abingdon   J5
Oxfordshire (pop. 18,610) There was once a Saxon abbey here, but only a few monastic buildings remain. The group round the guildhall includes the 15th-century main gateway to the abbey, 12th-century St John's Hospital (used as a Court since 1560) and medieval St Nicholas Church, originally built for abbey tenants and guests. Until 1867, Abingdon was Berkshire's county town, which accounts for fine buildings like County Hall (built 1678), today housing a local history museum. Thames Street features a 14th-century watermill and, opposite Thames Street, is the 19th-century jail, built by Napoleonic war prisoners, now imaginatively converted to a leisure centre.

Because of its excellent ford, **Wallingford** 13km/8mi SE, was always at the heart of historic events; today that same crossing-place is spanned by one of the finest bridges of the Thames. The railway town of **Didcot** lies 8km/5mi SE; steam locomotives and rolling stock are on display at the Railway Centre.

Banbury   F4
Oxfordshire (pop. 29,387) Banbury is an excellent base for touring the Oxfordshire Cotswolds and visiting mellow stone villages like Deddington, Bloxham and Adderbury. Banbury is also a leading agricultural centre; the Thursday market is Europe's most important cattle market. Look out for the Banbury Cross of nursery-rhyme fame, and sample delicious Banbury Cakes, made of pastry filled with dried spiced fruit. Banbury Museum shows local history exhibits, while **Cropredy**, 6km/4mi N, retains tangible evidence of the Civil War – armour, bayonets, cannon-balls – in the 14th-century church.

Bedford   E10
Bedfordshire (pop. 73,229) The county town of Bedfordshire straddles the River Great Ouse. Bedford is proud of its connections with the religious writer, **John Bunyan**, who lived here from 1655 until his death in 1688. Among many reminders are the John Bunyan Meeting Library and Museum, containing personal relics, and a collection of his work in over 150 languages. Cecil Higgins Art Gallery has an excellent display of 18th-century ceramics, glass, furniture, silver and English watercolours. **Elstow**, 3km/2mi S, was John Bunyan's home village; the 16th-century Moot Hall (market hall) has a rural life exhibition showing Bedfordshire in Bunyan's day. May Day (1 May) is celebrated with maypole dancing on the green.

Henley-on-Thames   L7
Oxfordshire (pop. 11,431) The first rowing regatta in the world was held in this picturesque Thames-side town in 1839, and is still held annually in July. Regatta Week is one of the highlights of England's social calendar and ranks with Ascot and Wimbledon as a sporting event. Henley's main street is elegantly Georgian and you can find several interesting old inns with bull and bear baiting yards. Kenton Theatre dates from 1805 and the Town Hall is Victorian. **Grey's Court**, 5km/3mi NW, is a gabled Elizabethan manor house. Henley is a good centre for visiting riverside villages like Hambleden, Medmenham, Sonning and Hurley.

High Wycombe   K9
Buckinghamshire (pop. 59,340) Although the town is greatly modernized, there are still old buildings of interest such as Little Market House (1761) and the 13th-century parish church. The **chairmaking** industry, for which High Wycombe is world-famous, was established in the 17th century. Wycombe Chair Museum displays local craftsmen's tools and examples of Chippendale, Hepplewhite, Sheraton and Windsor furniture. **Hughenden Manor**, 3km/2mi N, was the home of Benjamin Disraeli, Prime Minister and friend of Queen Victoria; it contains his furniture, pictures and books.

The pretty National Trust village of **West Wycombe**, 5km/3mi W, is still the family seat of Sir Francis Dashwood, Premier Baronet of England. The house is set in 120 hectares/300 acres and contains notable furnishings. To the north are the notorious **Hell Fire Caves**, the mausoleum and church topped by an immense golden ball, inside which convened the 18th-century Hell Fire Club – aristocrats who dabbled in Satanism.

The 16th-century half-timbered cottage, where the poet **John Milton** lived while the Plague of 1665 raged in London, can be visited at Chalfont St Giles, 13km/8mi E. Here he completed his epic poem *Paradise Lost* and began writing *Paradise Regained*. Milton relics are on display, including first editions of both poems.

Jordans K10

Buckinghamshire This peaceful village is famous for its Quaker associations. Old Jordans is the original farmhouse in which the Quakers met despite harsh opposition from the law; it is now a residential retreat (exterior only can be viewed). Outside the Quaker meeting house (built 1688), are the simple gravestones of the family of **William Penn**, the leading Quaker, and founder of Pennsylvania, USA. See also the Mayflower Barn, reputed to be made of oak timbers from the ship which took the Pilgrim Fathers to America.

Luton H11

Bedfordshire (pop. 161,405) This industrial town was famous for straw-plaiting and straw hat-making, which began in the 17th century, now mainly replaced by other trades. The Victorian mansion, Wardown, is an art gallery and museum.

Luton Hoo, 3km/2mi S, houses the world-famous Wernher Collection of priceless objects made by Peter Fabergé, jeweller to the last Czar of Russia. Ayot St Lawrence, 11km/7mi SE, was the home of the Irish dramatist **George Bernard Shaw**. Shaw's Corner, his home from 1906–50, is set out as it was in his lifetime. **Whipsnade Zoo**, 10km/6mi SW, close to Dunstable Downs, houses over 2000 animals.

From Luton you might visit **Knebworth House** and Country Park, 16km/10mi E, home of the Lytton family from 1492 to the present day; it has a magnificent Tudor banqueting hall, furniture, paintings, and other treasures covering 500 years of English history. **Hitchin**, 13km/8mi NE of Knebworth, is an interesting town whose medieval streets, such as Tilehouse Street, are worth exploring on foot.

Marlow K8

Buckinghamshire (pop. 10,350) This busy town has a beautiful riverside setting with 19th-century suspension bridge, bankside All Saints parish church and world-famous **Compleat Angler** hotel. Many attractive Georgian houses can be seen in the High Street and also West Street – where the poets Shelley and T.S. Eliot and the novelist Thomas Love Peacock lived.

Cookham, 5km/3mi SE, was the home of the painter **Stanley Spencer**, and his work and personal effects can be seen in the Stanley Spencer Gallery in the Kings Hall. **Cliveden House**, 6km/4mi SE, was built in 1850; the gardens, which contain temples and Roman sarcophagi, are remarkable for their woodland walks and river views.

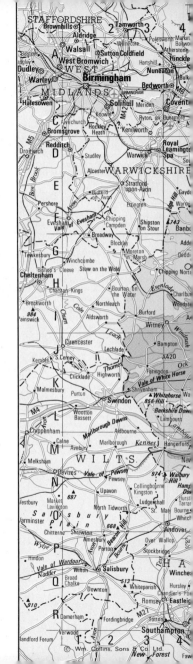

The Chiltern Hills

Newbury   M5

Berkshire (pop. 23,643) You'll see race-horses exercising on the Berkshire Downs surrounding this busy town, and there's a racecourse close by. The Museum houses prehistoric finds and Civil War relics in a restored 17th-century Cloth Hall; more evidence of Civil War sieges can be found 3km/2mi NW at **Donnington Castle**, a late 14th-century gatehouse with earth-works.

Take a towpath stroll beside the Kennet and Avon canal or, more romantically, travel in a horse-drawn barge (details from the Thames and Chilterns Tourist Board, address on p. 26). The canal runs along to **Hungerford** 13km/8mi W, a pretty riverside town bursting with an-tique shops. Fine collections of Civil War armour are displayed in **Littlecote House**, a Tudor manor, 5km/3mi NW of Hungerford; the Cromwellian Chapel is one of the best examples of the period.

From Newbury you might visit **Lam-bourn**, famous for its training stables, 19km/12mi NW, beside Lambourn Downs, and the **White Horse of Uffing-ton**, 24km/15mi NW, a chalk figure cut into the hillside a thousand years ago.

Oxford   I5

Oxfordshire (pop. 108,805) Most of the colleges in this ancient and beautiful uni-versity city can be visited: University College (founded 1249) is the oldest, while Merton College (founded 1264) has England's oldest library. New College dates from 1379; Christ Church was founded in 1525 by Cardinal Wolsey; Magdalen (pronounced 'Maudlin') Col-lege was largely built in the 15th century and Trinity College a century later.

Churches to visit include Christ Church Cathedral, formerly an Augus-tinian Priory and noted for its stained glass, and the University Church of St Mary the Virgin, now the home of a brass rubbing centre. Oxford's outstanding museums include the Ashmolean Museum (Britain's first public museum), the Museum of the History of Science, and the Museum of Modern Art. The Sheldonian Theatre, built 1664–9 by Sir Christopher Wren, is mainly used for university ceremonies.

Like the students, you too can go punting on the River Cherwell which winds through Oxford, or enjoy lovely riverside walks. Another peaceful place is the University Botanic Gardens, founded in 1621.

St Albans   J11

Hertfordshire (pop. 52,174) The Romans built their city, Verulamium, here in AD 43. Roman remains include a hypocaust (heating system) and theatre, with other items in the Museum. The cathedral, St Albans Abbey, is the second longest church in Britain. Inside is the shrine of St Alban, Britain's first Christian martyr; also fine medieval wall paintings. Fishpool Street contains interesting houses and nearby is French Row with its timber-framed 15th- and 16th-century houses. The 15th-century clock tower, one of only two in England, offers fine views.

Hatfield House, 8km/5mi NE, a magnificent Jacobean house, home of the Marquess of Salisbury, was built in 1607–11 by Robert Cecil and contains furniture, portraits and relics of Queen Elizabeth I.

Windsor   M9

Berkshire (pop. 30,114) Windsor Castle was founded by William the Conqueror, and is the largest inhabited residence in the world. It has been a royal residence since Henry I's reign in the 12th century, and incorporates additions dating from that time to the reign of Queen Victoria. St George's Chapel (now a royal burial place) is the finest example of Perpendicular architecture in England. You can look round the famous Round Tower state apartments and see the daily Changing of the Guard. The Castle is surrounded by the 1940-hectare/4800-acre Great Park in which Queen Elizabeth often rides.

The town is largely Victorian with some Georgian buildings. An enjoyable evening can be spent at the delightful Theatre Royal: other places to visit are the Royalty and Empire Exhibition, open daily at Central Station; The **Savill Garden**, 6km/4mi S, and **Windsor Safari Park** 3km/2mi S. **Eton College**, famous public school, founded in 1440 by Henry VI, lies on the farther bank of the River Thames.

Woodstock   I4

Oxfordshire (pop. 1961) Blenheim Palace dominates this tiny, charming town. It was built (1705–22) by the English architect and dramatist Sir John Vanbrugh, and given by Queen Anne to the Duke of Marlborough to celebrate his victory at Blenheim in 1704. It contains notable furnishings and is set in a 810-hectare/2000-acre park. **Sir Winston Churchill**, the English statesman and wartime premier, was born here in 1874; he was buried in 1965 in the village churchyard of Bladon on the park's southern fringe.

All Souls College, Oxford

Windsor Castle

EAST ANGLIA

East Anglia's attraction lies in its undramatic but subtle landscapes. Wherever you go, you're never far from water – inland lakes, rivers, fen canals, the sea – nor from the countryside.

The 14th, 15th and 16th centuries were East Anglia's main periods of prosperity; most of Cambridge's colleges were founded then and other buildings throughout the area sprang up: solid stone guildhalls, manor houses, thatched inns. Because the towns largely escaped the influence of the Industrial Revolution, you can still see Norman castles, medieval churches, Tudor timbered houses and 18th-century mansions much as they always were.

Seek out those little Essex villages which generally get overlooked; in particular Thaxted with its fine church, Finchingfield and the collective groups of villages called The Rodings and The Easters. Then there are the 'field' villages: Great and Little Bardfield, Toppesfield, Wethersfield. Saffron Walden and Braintree are larger centres; both a jumble of historic inns, modern shopping centres and Victorian public buildings. As for the Essex seaside resorts, Southend's 11km/7mi seafront is within a day-trip of London; Clacton caters for most tastes in its entertainment programme, while next-door Frinton is altogether more restrained.

The main Eastern railway line serves Colchester, Norwich and Ipswich. South of Colchester lie marshes and estuaries, haunt of gull, lapwing and coot. Maldon, Tollesbury and Burnham-on-Crouch are the main marshland villages which double as boating centres. North of Colchester lies Dedham Vale, home of the 18th-century landscape artist, Constable.

Using Ipswich as a base, you could motor north along the Suffolk coastline to Aldeburgh, home of the poet George Crabbe whose work *The Borough* was inspiration for the opera *Peter Grimes*. Its composer, Benjamin Britten, lived here until his death in 1976; his works are performed at the annual Aldeburgh Festival in June. Further north, explore the Georgian buildings of gracious Southwold.

Your return trip to Ipswich might take in the Georgian mansion Heveningham Hall, near Halesworth; Laxfield, with its thatched and timbered houses and church tower which displays the flint and limestone panelling called 'flushwork'; 18th-century Saxtead Green Post Mill, still in full working order; Framlingham, with its giant castle and Perpendicular St Michael's Church; and Woodbridge, an old-world market town on the River Deben.

The Rivers Orwell and Stour flow into the sea near Felixstowe, a popular resort which, like Lowestoft further north, offers seaside attractions as well as being a ferry and container port. On the outskirts of Lowestoft is Oulton Broad, a busy stretch of water which forms a gateway to the Norfolk Broads.

Over 160km/100mi of navigable waterway make up The Broads – an area of reed-fringed lakes, many of which are linked by rivers. There are no locks and little tide for sailors to worry about, and plenty of wildlife and waterfowl to observe. The area is best explored by boat: various craft can be rented from centres such as Horning, Hickling, Oulton Broad, Beccles and Wroxham.

Inland, around the cathedral city of Norwich, there are neat villages and market towns like Wymondham (pronounced 'Windham'), with its market cross and overhanging cottages. A few miles west at Hingham, Abraham Lincoln's family lived for many generations until they emigrated to America in 1637. Thetford is part of an area called Breckland. 'Brecks' were tracts of heath, spasmodically broken up for cultivation by early man, but allowed to relapse into wildness. Today the area is well covered by pine forests and is rich in archaeological finds.

The best-known part of East Anglia is the marshlands called The Fens, drained in the 17th and 18th centuries by Dutch engineers using a system of canals. Main centres for Fenland are Ely, where Hereward the Wake, leader of the Anglo-Saxons, made his stand against Norman invaders led by William the Conqueror; the cathedral city of Peterborough; the market town of Wisbech; and Huntingdon where Oliver Cromwell was brought up and which has an excellent museum devoted to him. Further south is Newmarket where race meetings are held from April to October, and the beautiful university city of Cambridge.

The centres best served by public transport in East Anglia are Cambridge and Norwich, but a good way to get around is on two wheels (few hills to negotiate!) and you'll find bicycle rental shops in Norwich, Cambridge, Ipswich and Colchester. If you want accommodation, head for these towns, also Newmarket, Bury St Edmunds, Woodbridge, King's Lynn and Cromer.

Pheasant and Plaice The rich, arable farmlands of East Anglia and its long coastline provide many a splendid dish. Norfolk Turkey and Norfolk Duckling are renowned for their quality, while pheasant, partridge and duck are all available in season. Colchester, Mersea and Barling are noted for oysters, Cromer for its crabs. Although herrings are not so plentiful as formerly, they are still landed at Lowestoft, along with local plaice. The traditional Lowestoft way with herring is to boil quickly (in sea water, if possible) and serve simply with boiled potatoes and a mustard sauce.

Inland, asparagus, strawberries and soft fruits are plenteous; Essex in particular is a jam-making centre. Most towns have open-air markets selling local produce; the finest is probably Norwich. As for beer, Greene King beers come from Bury St Edmunds, Adnams from Southwold and Tolly Cobbold from Ipswich in Suffolk.

Festivals and Events Early Jan., Norwich Antiques Fair. Mid-March, National Shire Horse Show – Peterborough. Mid-May, Felixstowe Folk Festival; end May, Suffolk Show – Ipswich. Early June, Thaxted Morris Ring; Cambridge University Footlights Review; end June, Aldeburgh Festival – Snape Maltings; Midsummer Fair – Cambridge; Colchester Rose Show; Royal Norfolk Show – Norwich; Lord Mayor's Procession – Norwich; mid-July, Cambridge Festival and Folk Festival; East of England Show – Peterborough; Colchester Carnival; end July, Sandringham Flower Show; King's Lynn Festival; Framlingham Lawn Tennis Tournament; Colchester Cricket Week; end Aug., Harlow Show. Late Sept., Benson & Hedges Chamber Music Festival – Snape Maltings. 5 Nov., Colchester Firework Display.

Bury St Edmunds   I7

Suffolk (pop. 25,661) For people who enjoy buildings and history, it's hard to improve upon Bury St Edmunds. The Abbey (now ruins) was built to house the shrine of King Edmund, murdered by the Danes. Norman Gate (built *ca*1120) and Abbey Gate (*ca*1430), together with the Cathedral Church of St James and St Mary's Church, form the heart of medieval Bury, with the River Lark flowing through grounds behind the Abbey. Moyse's Hall, now a museum, dates from the 12th century. Angel Corner, an 18th-century house, contains the Gershom Parkington clock collection.

Within easy reach are the old wool towns of **Long Melford**, 19km/12mi S, and **Lavenham** 16km/10mi SE, while at Sudbury, 24km/15mi S, you can visit the birthplace of the 18th-century artist **Gainsborough**.

Cambridge   I3

Cambridgeshire (pop. 98,840) This beautiful county town has one of the two oldest universities in England. The first scholars came in 1209 from Oxford, but it was not until 1284 that the first college, Peterhouse, was founded. Clare, Pembroke, Trinity Hall and Corpus Christi Colleges were all founded in the 14th century. King's College Chapel retains all its medieval stained glass and contains Ruben's famous painting *The Adoration of the Magi*. Guided tours of the colleges are available from the Tourist Information Centre, Bene't Street. The Fitzwilliam Museum is well worth visiting, especially for the excellent Egyptology section; also the Scott Polar Research Institute, a museum of polar exploration and research; Cambridge and County Folk Museum; and Cambridge Holographics exhibition.

Cambridge has a wide variety of good shops, lovely parks, riverside walks and a Botanic Garden. Punts can be rented at Magdalene (pronounced 'Maudlin') Bridge for a trip past the Backs: lawns behind the colleges sloping to the river.

Colchester   M8

Essex (pop. 76,531) Colchester is England's oldest recorded town. The Romans built a great fortress city here and parts of the Roman walls remain, including high Balkerne Gate. Castle Museum contains an outstanding collection of Romano-British antiquities in 11th-century Colchester Castle, which has one of Europe's largest keeps. An 18th-century house contains the Minories Art Gallery, while a costume collection is displayed in the Georgian house, Holly-

82

trees. Over the centuries, Colchester has been a great weaving centre and the heart of the oyster trade – there's a unique oyster feast in October.

Dedham Vale — L9

Essex The countryside surrounding Dedham village has been immortalized in the paintings of landscape artist, **John Constable**, who was born, in 1776, in a house above Dedham Vale. His father owned two windmills near East Bergholt and watermills at Flatford and Dedham. In paintings like *The Haywain* and *Flatford Mill* he reflected the pastoral beauty of his home surroundings.

Ely — G4

Cambridgeshire (pop. 9020) Ely is dominated by its magnificent cathedral, begun in 1083 on the site of a 7th-century Benedictine Abbey. The wonderful octagon lantern, added in the 14th century, was one of the finest engineering feats of the Middle Ages. There's an enjoyable walk from the cathedral to Cherry Hill Park along the banks of the River Ouse.

Ipswich — K10

Suffolk (pop. 123,312) This thriving port on the River Orwell is also Suffolk's county town. By the Middle Ages, Ipswich had become one of Britain's most successful trading ports. Like King's Lynn and Norwich, it was once the home of rich merchants – walk round the old town and see the results. Cardinal Wolsey was born in Ipswich, and Chaucer's father used to trade here. Ancient House (built 1567) in Butter Market has fine pargeting on the walls. (Pargeting is a type of decorated plasterwork seen at its best in East Anglia.) Christchurch Mansion is a lively domestic museum.

The Museum of East Anglian Life at **Stowmarket**, 19km/12mi NW, is an agricultural collection housed in a medieval barn. From Ipswich you can easily reach **Felixstowe**, 18km/11mi SE, a 19th-century seaside resort with a Martello Tower (built *ca*1810), and the old port of Harwich.

King's Lynn — D5

Norfolk (pop. 30,107) This ancient market town and port was once called Bishop's Lynn, but was renamed when Henry VIII took over the Bishop's Manor. St George's Guildhall (15th-century), now a theatre, is the largest surviving English medieval guildhall. See also the Holy Trinity Guildhall and many other buildings dating from medieval to Georgian times. At the Lynn Museum, a display of medieval pilgrims' badges is of

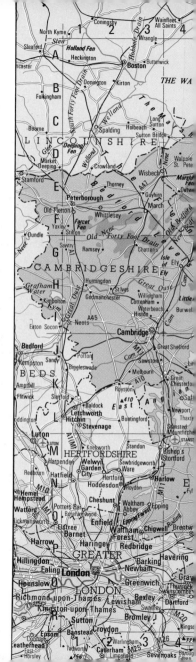

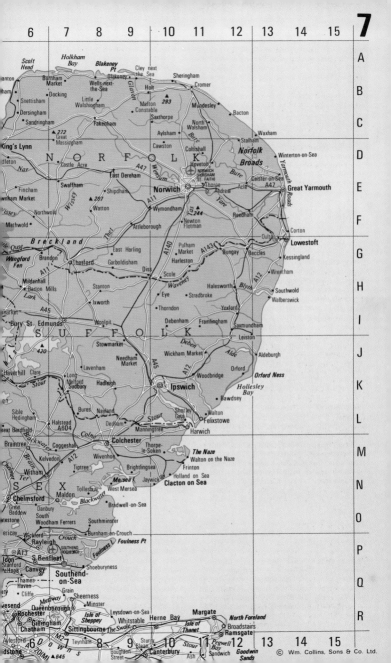

Sandringham House, Norfolk

special interest, while the Museum of Social History shows costumes, glass and toys. The Tuesday market has been held since the 12th century and Saturday's market is even older. **Sandringham Gardens**, 13km/8mi NE, is a 2830-hectare/7000-acre estate owned by the royal family; the grounds are open if no member of the family is in residence.

Newmarket   I5
Suffolk (pop. 9900) James I was the first king to visit Newmarket, partly because the hunting was so good, but it was his Scottish nobles who introduced racing. Charles II also encouraged the sport, and Newmarket has remained a popular horse racing and breeding centre – see the handsome building of the Jockey Club in the High Street and the National Horse-racing Museum. Nell Gwyn's cottage (exterior only can be viewed) escaped the fire of 1683 which consumed many older buildings. The Bushel Inn, off Market Street, retains its original cockpit.

Norwich   E10
Norfolk (pop. 122,083) Norwich retains a picture-book atmosphere, with its castle (built *ca* 1160), Norman cathedral, 33 medieval churches and the River Wensum. Castle Museum; Strangers Hall Museum (domestic life); Bridewell Museum (local industries and crafts); St Peter Hungate Museum (church art) are all worth seeing. Norwich is the home of Colman's Mustard and the Mustard Shop in Bridewell Alley sells many varieties.

Norwich is a good centre for boating on the Broads, and it is possible to travel by water all the way to **Great Yarmouth**, 29km/18mi E.

Saffron Walden   K4
Essex (pop. 9971) Few English towns have retained their medieval street layouts as clearly as Saffron Walden. The town's origins date from the Neolithic and Bronze Ages, but it principally prospered in the Middle Ages through the wool trade and the crop of saffron (used as a medicine

and dye). Markets are held on Tuesday and Saturday and the Market Place has many interesting buildings, including the Town Hall (1762) and the Corn Exchange (1850). The Sun Inn, Church Street, was reputedly occupied by Oliver Cromwell during the Civil War. The Museum exhibits archaeology and natural history. Visit St Mary's Church, one of the largest in Essex; also **Audley End House**, 1½km/1mi W, built 1603. The present interior and grounds are largely the late 18th-century work of the architect Robert Adam, who took care to preserve their Jacobean elegance.

Southend-on-Sea   Q7
Essex (pop. 162,770) Only 58km/36mi from London, Southend is one of England's biggest seaside resorts. The 11km/7mi seafront ranges from the old-fashioned seaside atmosphere and fishing boats at Leigh-on-Sea to the more sophisticated air of the Western Esplanade. The Historic Aircraft Museum and 14th-century timber-framed South Church Hall are worth visiting. You can buy cockles and other seafood at Leigh-on-Sea Cockle Sheds, 3km/2mi W.

Thetford   G7
Norfolk (pop. 13,727) Thetford lies beside the Rivers Thet and Little Ouse alongside an area of forests and sandy heaths called Breckland. It is one of the few towns in Britain to have Anglo-Saxon remains and the castle – one of the original motte-and-bailey castles – shows the earliest form of fortification before masonry was added. See also Thetford Priory, the remains of a 12th-century Cluniac monastery. Timbered, 15th-century Ancient House is now a museum of Breckland life, while White Hart Street contains the birthplace of **Thomas Paine**, author of *The Rights of Man*. Thetford Forest is one of England's largest man-made forests, with picnic areas, walks and nature trails. **Grimes Graves**, 8km/5mi NW, are Neolithic flint-mines, one of which you can inspect.

Thurne Mill on the Norfolk Broads

River Cam and the Bridge of Sighs, Cambridge

THE SHIRES

Good sunshine records and miles of un-blemished beaches attract holidaymakers to the Lincolnshire coast, to cheerful Skegness and Mablethorpe and to restful Sutton-on-Sea and Chapel St Leonards. Moving inland across the high, rolling chalklands of the Lincolnshire Wolds, golden with grain in summer, you'll see the landscape much as the poet Tennyson saw it over 100 years ago. Nothing here has changed much since Tennyson was born at Somersby (NE of Horncastle) in 1809 and spent his schooldays in Louth.

Tour round the triangle formed by Louth, Horncastle and Spilsby and absorb the timelessness of churches and hamlets like Oxcombe, Farforth and Ruckland. There are antiquities too, Bronze-Age long barrows, Iron-Age hill forts, Roman roads and the medieval villages deserted in Tudor times (there are five in a 8km/5mi stretch west of Louth). Lincoln, with its glimpses of the past – a medieval cathedral, a Norman bridge, a Roman arch – makes a good touring centre.

Nottinghamshire is the home of Sher-wood Forest, inseparable from tales of its legendary folk-hero, Robin Hood. The Forest is less extensive than at the time when the outlaw spent his days robbing the rich to give to the poor. Even so, there's plenty of woodland and rural scenes with Robin Hood displays at the Sher-wood Forest Visitor Centre.

The Peak District was England's first National Park. This area of rugged moor-land is roughly 48km/30mi long, 32km/20mi wide and 610m/2000ft at its highest points. The northern area is called the 'Dark Peak' because of its characteristic gritstone rock, but around Baslow the gritstone gives way to gleaming limestone which has christened the southern area the 'White Peak'. This part is more pas-toral, with Dovedale one of England's outstanding beauty spots.

The most challenging walks are around the High Peak area, which is also the beginning of the Pennine Way, a 400km/250mi footpath stretching north to the Scottish border. A good way to explore the High Peak and Derbyshire Dales is by walking, riding or cycling (bicycle rental available) along the High Peak or Tissing-ton Trails, following former railway lines. Buxton makes a good centre; also Ash-bourne, home of the famous Shrovetide football game and noted for gingerbread.

This area is graced with solid, stately homes: Chatsworth (p. 87); medieval Haddon Hall (3km/2mi SE of Bakewell); Sudbury Hall (8km/5mi SE of Uttoxeter) with its Museum of Childhood; formal gardens at Melbourne Hall (11km/7mi SE of Derby); and Robert Adam's Kedleston Hall (6km/4mi NW of Derby).

Keep an eye out in the Derbyshire villages for 'well dressing' a custom, dating from pagan times, in which village wells are decorated with intricate pictures made of petals, seeds and bark pressed into a clay base. The ritual is said to have originated in Tissington (6km/4mi N of Ashbourne), where it takes place on Ascension Day; other villages celebrate at different times, May–September.

Moving south, you come to another 'forest', the rocky outcrops of Leicester-shire's Charnwood Forest (8km/5mi SW of Loughborough), now pleasantly wood-ed. The scenery settles even more gently on the eye in the eastern part of Leicester-shire, although there are still castles to visit like Belvoir (19km/12mi NE of Melton Mowbray). South again, more historic houses – Althorp, family home of the Princess of Wales, Boughton House, Rockingham Castle – and fine churches make Northamptonshire an interesting county to explore.

Cheese and Ale The traditional dining-table of the Shires reflects the presence of the English landed gentry over the cen-turies. Sporting specialities abound in this fox-hunting area: Game Soup is thick and flavoured with port wine, while Melton Hunt Cake is still made to a 120-year-old recipe. Melton Mowbray pork pies come from the area, along with other pork specialities (haslet, brawn and pork fag-gots), and Red Leicester and Stilton cheeses. Notably popular ales are brewed at the Ruddles Brewery, Oakham; there is also a draught Rutland Barley Wine.

Bakewell Pudding reputedly originated

from the Rutland Arms Hotel in Bakewell when a customer ordered strawberry tart and the cook mistakenly spread egg-mixture on top of the jam instead of using it in the pastry! Bakewell Pudding can be bought and eaten at The Old Pudding Shop, Bakewell.

Regional markets selling food include Chesterfield, Leicester, Mansfield, North-ampton, Melton Mowbray and Louth.

Festivals and Events Early May, Spalding Flower Parade; Lincoln Festival; Ascension Day, Well Dressing – Tissington; end May, Well Dressing – Wirksworth. June, Nottingham Festival; Boston Festival; Lincoln Water Festival; Lincoln Wine Festival; end June, Well Dressing in Rowsley, Hope, Bakewell, Early July, Hathersage Gala; Market Bosworth Show; Well Dressing – Buxton; end July, Buxton Festival, Northampton Show. Aug. (first week), Bakewell Show; mid-Aug., Louth Flower and Produce Show; end Aug., Grand Transport Extravaganza – Crich; Well Dressing – Eyam. Early Sept., Burghley Horse Trials. Early Oct., Chatsworth Horse Trials; Goose Fair – Nottingham.

Buxton   E1

Derbyshire (pop. 20,324) At 305m/1000ft above sea level, this is one of England's highest towns and one of its oldest spas. The Romans first discovered the curative powers of the chalybeate springs. The graceful Crescent was built in the 18th century, when Buxton vied with Bath to be the more fashionable spa. Today you can still take the waters or swim in them in the public pool. In July/August the superbly restored Edwardian Opera House comes into its own during the Buxton Festival.

This is an excellent touring centre for the **Peak District National Park** and for visiting delightful Derbyshire villages like **Hope**, 16km/10mi NE, **Baslow**, 19km/12mi E, **Hathersage**, 19km/12mi NE, (where Jane Eyre 'lived') and **Bakewell**, 18km/11mi SE, (home of the famous pudding). At **Castleton**, 13km/8mi NE, you can explore the underground caverns where the rare mineral 'Blue John' is mined. The name comes from the French description *bleu-jaune*, and jewellery made from this translucent variety of fluorspar can be bought at the caverns and in Castleton.

Chesterfield   E4

Derbyshire (pop. 70,169) The crooked spire (70m/228ft) of the 14th-century Church of St Mary and All Saints is the most famous landmark of this ancient town, whose history is also shown in old

street names like The Shambles, Packer's Row and Knifesmithgate. At Old Whittingdon is the Revolution House, now a museum, where the Earl of Devonshire and his fellow conspirators plotted, in 1688, to overthrow James II and put William of Orange on the throne. Chesterfield has links with **George Stephenson**, inventor of the steam engine, who is buried in Holy Trinity Church.

Chatsworth House, 13km/8mi W, is a beautiful mansion packed with art and furnishings. **Hardwick Hall**, a supreme example of Elizabethan architecture, built *ca* 1595, lies 13km/8mi SE.

Derby   H3

Derbyshire (pop. 219,582) Derby is the home of Rolls-Royce and Royal Crown Derby: historic aero-engines are displayed in the Old Silk Mill, while the porcelain is on show in the City Museum. Derby is a good base for visiting **Melbourne** (13km/8mi S) with its fine Hall and gardens and Norman Church, or to ride on some of the 40 tramcars in the delightful **Tramway Museum** at Crich 19km/12mi N.

Leicester   K6

Leicestershire (pop. 284,208) The 2nd-century Roman baths and Jewry Wall are evidence of this county town's long history. Newarke Houses Museum provides a comprehensive guide to Leicestershire's social history, while Wygston's House displays English costume from 1760–1920. The Magazine, an ancient city gateway, is now a Museum of the Royal Leicestershire Regiment. The 15th-century timbered guildhall is well preserved; older still is St Nicholas' Church, whose history dates back to Saxon times. A daily market has been held near the old Corn Exchange since the 13th century.

Bosworth Battlefield at Sutton Cheney, 22km/14mi SW, is the site where Henry Tudor's defeat of Richard III, in 1485, ended the Wars of the Roses and founded the Tudor dynasty. The Visitor Centre and Battlefield Trails explain the course of events.

Lincoln   E9

Lincolnshire (pop. 74,269) One of Britain's most historically important cities. The oldest part is situated north of the River Witham which surrounds the 11th-century castle and Lincoln Cathedral – a superb example of Early English architecture, breathtakingly floodlit at night.

More ancient than the famous Jews' Houses (both of which date back to the 12th century) is Newport Arch, built by the Romans in the 2nd century. The half-timbered shops near the High Bridge (itself a 12th-century construction) remain much as they were in the 16th century. City and County Museum illustrates local archaeology, while the Museum of Lincolnshire Life shows the county's domestic and agricultural past.

Louth C13

Lincolnshire (pop. 11,170) This beautifully preserved Georgian town is set at the eastern end of the peaceful, rolling Lincolnshire Wolds. You'll see a variety of 18th- and 19th-century architecture by wandering round the narrow, winding streets of old houses, shops and inns, and a fine example of late Gothic work – the Perpendicular-style Church of St James. Louth is recorded in the Domesday Book (1086) and has always been Lincolnshire's busiest market town (held Fridays).

Northampton O7

Northamptonshire (pop. 151,000) The county capital and market town. Among its interesting churches is one of only four remaining round churches in England, the Holy Sepulchre, built *ca* 1100 by a Crusader returning from the Holy Land. Others to see are Norman-style St Peters and 14th-century All Saints. The Museum of Leathercraft indicates the importance of shoe manufacture in the locality. Seventh-century **Brixworth Church**, 10km/6mi N, is of note; also the Saxon church at **Earls Barton**, 11km/7mi NE, not far from the fine Elizabethan Mansion, **Castle Ashby**, to the south.

Nottingham H6

Nottinghamshire (pop. 300,630) This busy commercial and university city is well known as the home of the legendary **Robin Hood**. The 'Trip to Jerusalem' claims to be England's oldest inn and is said to have been visited by Crusaders en route for the Holy Land. The present Nottingham Castle dates from the 17th century and houses works of art; nearby are Brewhouse Yard Museum of Nottingham Life and the Costume Museum. The Industrial Museum details Nottingham's varied industries, other aspects of which are demonstrated at the **Papplewick Pumping Station** (13km/8mi N) and at **Ruddington Framework Knitters' Museum** (6km/4mi S). Visit also **Wollaton Hall**, an Elizabethan mansion, 5km/3mi W, **Southwell Minster**, 19km/12mi NE and **Newstead Abbey**, 14km/9mi N, home of poet **Lord Byron**.

Eastwood, 10km/6mi NW, was the

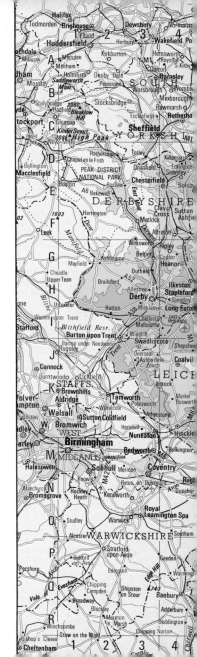

home of the author **D.H. Lawrence**. He was born at 8a Victoria Street, now re-fitted to look as it did at his birth. The surrounding area provides the setting for his Nottinghamshire/Derbyshire novels.

Spalding   J12
Lincolnshire (pop. 15,850) This is the centre of England's bulb-growing indus-try and in springtime, masses of tulips, daffodils and hyacinths blaze with colour. Visit Springfields Show Gardens, a unique 8-hectare/20-acre flower spectacle and if you're here in May, don't miss the magnificent Flower Parade.

The 'Boston Stump' (the 83m/272ft high tower of St Botolph's Church) can be seen miles before you reach **Boston**, 26km/16mi NE. It was here, in 1607, that some of the first **Pilgrim Fathers** were arrested during an abortive attempt to escape religious persecution and reach Holland; their cells can still be seen in the 15th-century guildhall. They eventually managed to sail across the Atlantic, foun-ding Boston, Massachusetts, in 1630.

Stamford   K10
Lincolnshire (pop. 14,662) The Romans had a camp in this country town; Saxons further developed it; Danes made it the capital of the Fens. Later still, Normans built a castle, traces of which remain. By the 12th century, Stamford was an im-portant wool centre and rich merchants built the Tudor houses, Queen Anne villas and Georgian mansions: you'll see over 500 buildings of architectural and historical importance here. Just outside Stamford, to the south east, is the Eliza-bethan splendour of **Burghley House**.

Oakham, 18km/11mi W in Leicester-shire, is a compact country town complete with stocks (old form of punishment) and butter cross in the market square. A Norman banqueting hall is all that re-mains of Oakham Castle, the walls of which are decorated with horseshoes paid as a toll by visiting royalty and peers of the realm since medieval times.

Famous for its pork pies and Stilton cheese, **Melton Mowbray** 29km/18mi NW, became a hunting centre in the 19th century. The Museum displays items linked with the production of Stilton, made locally in the Vale of Belvoir, an attractive area guarded by **Belvoir Castle**.

Fox hunt in the Vale of Belvoir

Chatsworth House, Derbyshire

THE ROSE COUNTIES

The 30-year battle called the Wars of the Roses, in which the two sides of the north country fought (1455–85) for the right to provide an English king, was given this title because both parties adopted the English rose as emblem: the House of Lancaster took a red rose, the York family a white rose. Today, much that is particularly English in landscape, custom, food and folklore, can still be found in the counties of Lancashire and Yorkshire.

The varied history of the Rose counties is reflected in its people. Although they are welded together in unmistakable northernness of speech and manner, the people of the cities, towns and dales each have their own distinctive dialect and way of life. A cheerful lack of self-consciousness is one of the most beguiling characteristics and making friends can be almost embarrassingly easy.

There are two National Parks in Yorkshire: the Moors and the Dales. The wild, heathery moors can be explored from stone-built towns like Helmsley, Malton, Pickering and Kirkbymoorside. From here you can visit the cairns and stone circles, which early man left to mystify us, near Danby and Shooting House Rigg, and the sentinel castles left by later settlers. Northallerton and Thirsk fringe the moors in the west: both market centres retain an air of former coaching days.

The Moors tumble across Yorkshire to the sea, where there are splendid cliffs and pretty sandy bays. In addition to historic sites and seaside resorts, you'll find that each cove, each village has its own flavour: Staithes, Port Mulgrave, peaceful Runswick Bay, a haven for artists, and the old smuggling village of Robin Hood's Bay.

The Dales are the setting for James Herriot's books about the life of a vet and for the associated TV series 'All Creatures Great and Small'. Herriot admits that Darrowby, the make-believe market town in the series, is 'a bit of Thirsk, something of Richmond, Leyburn and Middleham'. Dales countryside is stunning: follow switchback hills into valleys occupied solely by Swaledale sheep; spin down open hillsides into characteristic stone villages like Askrigg and Wensley. Climb moorland peaks for sweeping views across soft, green valleys, patterned by dry-stone walls. Stretch your legs on the Pennine Way, a long-distance footpath curving right through the Dales.

In the southernmost dales and moorlands, around Brontë Country, you're never far from the amenities and accommodation of major towns and cities, such as the old wool and steel towns of Bradford, Leeds and Sheffield.

And on the western side of the country, the craggy hills and flouncing valleys of the Peak District remain satisfyingly remote, although they are within only 32km/20mi of cities like Sheffield and Manchester.

The industrial towns of Blackburn, Bolton, Nelson and Burnley, with varied accommodation, make good bases for trips round the western slopes of the Pennines. High on the hills you'll find sturdy country pubs in surprising places and some fine Northern beers, while miles of footpaths and bridleways will tempt you through a setting of heather and wild bilberries. Keep an eye open for local events in the villages and small towns – flower shows, cattle auctions, rural markets are all worth a visit.

The traditional English pleasures of the seaside resort – the Punch and Judy show, the piers, promenade, donkey-rides and candy-floss – can all be enjoyed on the Lancashire coast. Blackpool has attracted holidaymakers for over a hundred years, while at quieter Fleetwood you can watch trawlers returning with their catch, or ferry across to Douglas, capital of the Isle of Man. (Details of the Isle of Man on p. 98.)

Beers and Black Pudding 'Apple Pie without cheese is like a kiss without a squeeze' runs an old Yorkshire saying, so try some creamy, crumbly Wensleydale cheese with your sweet. Other Yorkshire delicacies include the huge Barnsley Chop (cut lengthwise across the saddle of lamb) and Yorkshire Pudding, a batter mixture traditionally roasted beneath a joint of beef, to allow the meat juices to flavour it. In addition to beef from the Dales and

lamb from the Moors, there is seafood from the ports – Whitby crab, Scarborough plaice and Grimsby haddock.

Masham is the home of Theakston's brewery whose renowned liquid, 'Old Peculier', is named after the local Church Court. Other local breweries include Sam Smith's of Tadcaster, Websters of Halifax and Joshua Tetley's of Leeds.

Remember to taste delicious Brontë liqueur before you head across to the North West, also good brewing country. Among the distinctive beers here are the two dark milds, the strong bitter and the old ale from Boddington's of Manchester.

Since the North West is a combination of industrial centres and dairy farmland, there is an emphasis on puddings, stews and casseroles – filling food for hard workers in a northern climate. Black Pudding, made of pigs' blood, oatmeal and onions can be eaten at breakfast or high tea (early-evening main meal). Another popular dish is Lancashire Hot Pot, containing lamb or mutton chops topped with a layer of potatoes. The rich farming area of Cheshire produces the famous cheese, whose origins date back to the 12th century.

Lancashire and Yorkshire manage to agree on one thing: Parkin (a cake made from ginger, flour and treacle) is a favourite in both counties.

Markets selling food include Bolton, Burnley (with its black pudding stalls), Chorley, Oldham, Preston, Wigan, Warrington, Barnsley, Bradford, Doncaster, Richmond, Ripon, Sheffield and Wakefield.

Festivals and Events Shrove Tuesday, Shrovetide Skipping Festival – Scarborough. Early April, Grand National Steeplechase – Aintree; Pageant of the Horse – Doncaster. Early May, Knutsford Royal May Day Festival; end May, Lancaster Military Tattoo; Chester Regatta; Planting of the Penny Hedge – Whitby; Humberside County Show – Beverley. Early June, Bramham Horse Trials – Wetherby; Morecambe Carnival; end June, Yn Chruinnaght (Manx Cultural Festival) – Ramsey, I.o.M.; Mayor's Parade – Manchester. Early July, West Lancashire Show – Skelmersdale; mid-July, Crewe and Nantwich Folk Festival; Masham Steam Engine and Fair Organ Rally. Early Aug., St Wilfrid's Feast – Ripon; end Aug., Whitby Folk Festival; Southport Flower Show; Bolton Festival (bi-annual, 1987, 1989). Mid-Aug. to Oct., Illuminations – Blackpool and Morecambe. Oct., Hull Fair. 24 Dec., Tolling of the Devil's Knell – Dewsbury; 26 Dec., Round the Walls running race – Chester.

Blackpool   I2

Lancashire (pop. 151,860) Funfair thrills from dodgem-cars to bingo and traditional seaside fare such as candy-floss and rock (confectionery) are found along the stretch of promenade known as the 'Golden Mile' and on the three piers of one of England's largest seaside resorts. The 10km/6mi promenade, well known for its autumn illuminations, is dominated by 158m/518ft Blackpool Tower, while electric trams running along the seafront are the only survivors of their kind in England. **Lytham St Annes** 10km/6mi S, is famous for its championship golf courses and sand-yacht races.

Bridlington   F20

Humberside (pop. 26,776) Bridlington Quay, the main focus of this busy fishing port and historic seaside resort, offers excellent sea-angling and the usual seaside amusements. At **Flamborough Head**, 8km/5mi E, where spectacular chalk cliffs rise some 122m/400ft above sea level, a memorial commemorates the famous naval battle here in which the American privateer, **John Paul Jones**, beat the British fleet during the War of American Independence.

Chester   P4

Cheshire (pop. 62,911) This old walled city has foundations dating back to Roman times. A Roman amphitheatre lies east of Newgate; other Roman remains are in the Grosvenor Museum. Much of the original Roman wall encircling the town survives; other towers and gates were added in the Middle Ages *ca*1400–1500. Also dating from this period are Chester's galleried streets, called 'The Rows', in which shops open on to balustraded walkways reached by steps from the road. Many half-timbered Tudor houses can be seen, notably Bishop Lloyd's House, God's Providence House and Old Leche House.

Both Chester Heritage Centre and Chester Visitor Centre provide a sight-and-sound reconstruction of the city's history. The Cathedral, originally an abbey dedicated to St Werburgh, still possesses features surviving from its monastic past. Chester Castle, built soon after the Norman Conquest, looks out across the River Dee towards Wales.

Clitheroe   I7

Lancashire (pop 13,194) A ruined Norman keep stands above the grey roofs of this pleasant market town, granted its charter in the 12th century. Other pretty villages in the Ribble Valley are **Downham**, 5km/3mi NE, and **Whalley**, 6km/4mi S, notable for the remains of its 13th-century Cistercian abbey. Pendle Hill (558m/1831ft) rises mysteriously 6km/4mi E; it was hereabouts that the famous Lancashire witches practised their magic in James I's reign.

Harrogate G12

North Yorkshire (pop. 62,427) Dignified Victorian architecture and well-planned parks and gardens characterize this stately 19th-century spa town. The first public spa baths, including the original sulphur well, were at the Royal Pump Room, now a local history museum; the Royal Bath Assembly Rooms are also worth visiting. Harrogate is the home of year-round entertainment, including music and drama festivals (Aug.) and the Great Yorkshire (agricultural) Show (July).

Georgian houses line the narrow streets of **Knaresborough**, 6km/4mi NE, while a ruined 14th-century castle crowns the clifftop. Paths lead through beech woods to the **Dropping Well** which petrifies any objects hung there. The legendary prophetess Mother Shipton was reputedly born (July 1488) in nearby **Mother Shipton's Cave.**

Haworth I9

West Yorkshire (pop. 3923) Haworth Parsonage, home of the 19th-century **Brontë** family of novelists – Charlotte, Emily and Anne – stands at the top of the main street in this moorland town. The Parsonage is now a museum displaying a collection of Brontë relics and manuscripts. The Black Bull Inn where their brother, Branwell, drank himself to death still stands; so does the bleak ruin of 'Top Withins' on the nearby moor – the reputed setting for Emily's novel *Wuthering Heights.* Walkers can follow the footsteps of the Brontës on the Brontë Way (21km/13mi) linking Haworth with Wycoller Hall over the moors in Lancashire. The Worth Valley Steam Railway, which trundles from Keighley to Oxenhope, stops at Haworth where there is a steam-engine collection.

Helmsley D15

North Yorkshire (pop. 1278) Charming grey stone houses with red roofs cluster round Helmsley's market square, not far from the ruins of its 12th-century castle. Helmsley has varied accommodation and is a good base for the North York Moors. The Cleveland Way, a long-distance footpath stretching to the coast, starts here.

Rievaulx Abbey is 5km/3mi NW. The name (pronounced 'Reevo') comes from 'Rye Vallis', or valley of the River Rye, above which the abbey ruins stand. It was founded in 1131 and is one of England's earliest Cistercian buildings; its chief glory is the choir, built ca1225.

Hull I20

Humberside (pop. 285,970) The confluence of the Rivers Hull and Humber has given rise to England's third largest port, whose official name is Kingston upon Hull. The magnificent Marina was opened in 1983, while the Town Docks Museum contains interesting exhibits relating to the sea. Wilberforce House is the birthplace of the famous 19th-century slave emancipator, **William Wilberforce**, while European Old Masters are on view in the Ferens Art Gallery.

Beverley, 13km/8mi N, is a flourishing market town with notable ecclesiastical architecture: 14th-century St Mary's Church and twin-towered 13th-century Beverley Minster. Beverley's market squares and narrow streets are distinguished by houses built during the prosperous days of the medieval cloth trade, The Museum of Army Transport is of interest to veterans and other enthusiasts.

Lancaster F4

Lancashire (pop. 49,584) The county town of Lancaster takes its name from a Roman camp built here, beside the River Lune. The imposing castle was a Parliamentary stronghold in the Civil War, but since the 18th century it has housed courts and a jail. A tree-lined quay is a reminder of the days when the city was an important port. The Customs House dates from the mid 18th century, while the Friends Meeting House was built in 1690.

The main street, Haworth

Spectacular views of the Lake District hills and fine sunsets across Morecambe Bay can be enjoyed at **Morecambe**, 6km/4mi W. This popular seaside town has plenty of accommodation and makes a base for nearby Lakeland countryside.

Leeds I12

West Yorkshire (pop. 496,009) Leeds grew up in the Industrial Revolution, and grand examples of Victorian architecture include the Town Hall and Municipal Buildings. Leeds offers excellent shopping facilities from quaint Victorian arcades to modern shopping centres and pedestrian precincts. Entertainment includes the famous City Varieties Music Hall, and English National Opera North at the Grand Theatre. Cricket enthusiasts should pay a visit to Headingley. Nearby is 12th-century Kirkstall Abbey and the Abbey House Museum with reconstructed period shops. **Temple Newsam House**, a splendid Tudor and Jacobean house, stands in parkland landscaped by Capability Brown, 3km/2mi SE.

The attractive market towns of Otley and Ilkley lie among the moors north west of Leeds. Otley Agricultural Show (May) claims to be the oldest of its kind, while the town's most famous inhabitant was **Thomas Chippendale**, the cabinetmaker, born here in 1718. Bird's-eye views of the moors can be had from Otley Chevin, 275m/900ft above the town.

Liverpool M3

Merseyside (pop. 610,113) Liverpool was first envisaged as a port at the turn of the 13th century when King John granted its charter. The 11km/7mi docks are best seen from the Mersey ferry or on a guided tour aboard a river barge (details from Tourist Information Centre). Be sure to see the new Merseyside Maritime Museum, modern Roman Catholic cathedral, the massive red sandstone Anglican cathedral, the Walker Art Gallery and Bluecoat Chambers, a lovely Queen Anne building; also visit the fabulous gardens (May–Sept), a permanent reminder of the 1984 International Garden Festival.

Speke Hall, 13km/8mi S, is a grand 16th-century, half-timbered Manor House.

Manchester L7

Greater Manchester (pop. 543,650) Manchester is connected to the Mersey by a ship canal, and is a thriving port as well as a centre for commerce, culture, sports and shopping. Apart from three excellent theatres, a cheap, noisy, friendly evening can be enjoyed at one of the 'Clubs', with their half-pub, half-nightclub atmosphere (details from Tourist Information Centre).

Manchester Cathedral was founded in 1421 and contains fine 15th-century woodwork and brasses. The city has some excellent museums and galleries: The City Art Gallery (pottery, pictures and silverware); Manchester Museum at The University (Ancient Egyptian exhibits); Whitworth Art Gallery (watercolours by Blake, Turner, Cezanne, Picasso); Greater Manchester Museum of Science and Industry (historical-industrial background); Manchester Air and Space Museum (aircraft). **Salford Art Gallery and Museum**, 3km/2mi W, has works by the 20th-century artist L.S. Lowry and 'Lark Hill Place' – a recreated street of shops and period rooms typical of a northern industrial town at the turn of the century.

Richmond C11

North Yorkshire (pop. 7245) Richmond Castle overlooks the Georgian and Victorian buildings grouped round the cobbled market place of this Swaledale town. Be sure to visit the Green Howards Museum, illustrating the history of this famous regiment, and The Georgian Theatre (built 1788). This is one of the oldest theatres in England still in use and famous performers, past and present, have included Edmund Kean and Yehudi Menuhin. **Easby Abbey**, 1½km/1mi E, was founded in 1155; remains include the gatehouse, chapter house and cloisters.

From Richmond, you can easily visit **Jervaulx Abbey**, 16km/10mi S, a ruined Cistercian monastery; **Middleham Castle**, 15km/9mi S, which was Richard III's favourite stronghold; **Castle Bolton**, 18km/11mi SW, where Mary, Queen of Scots was once imprisoned. **Aysgarth**, 22km/14mi SW, with its series of waterfalls and **Hawes**, 32km/20mi SW, famous for Wensleydale cheese, are also worth visiting.

Ripon F12

North Yorkshire (pop. 10,989) The market square is the focal point of this old town. Each evening, a forest horn is sounded, as in ancient times, by the Ripon Wakeman; his 13th-century Wakeman's House contains a small museum. Ripon Cathedral is particularly noted for its Norman Transitional north transept, its Early English west front (1220) and carved oak choir-stalls.

The magical ruins of **Fountains Abbey** lie 5km/3mi SW. It was founded in the 12th century and, through the wooltrading skills of its monks, became England's wealthiest Cistercian house.

Scarborough D19

North Yorkshire (pop. 44,440) Scarborough was one of the first English seaside resorts, made popular by 18th-century visitors who came to take the waters for the sake of their health. The headland is crowned by a ruined 12th-century castle overlooking the boats nosing in and out of the busy harbour. Scarborough is the venue for all kinds of events (cricket, fishing, motorcycling) throughout the year and there is a variety of nightlife. The town has one of the few traditional spa orchestras.

Whitby B18

North Yorkshire (pop. 12,150) This fishing port and seaside resort was once the home of navigator and explorer, **Captain Cook**. The harbour is ringed by hillside cottages and steep passages in which fishermen mend nets and little shops sell various craft wares. The headland is crowned by ruined 13th-century Whitby Abbey which stands on the site of a former 7th-century abbey, once the home of Caedmon, the first English Christian poet. A cross commemorating him stands nearby in St Mary's churchyard. Whitby

Beck Hole on the North York Moors

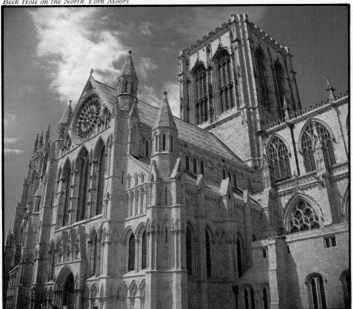

York Minster

is a handy base for exploring picturesque coves and fishing villages like **Ravenscar** 13km/8mi SE, **Robin Hood's Bay** 8km/ 5mi SE and **Staithes** 14km/9mi NW.

York   G15
North Yorkshire (pop. 104,782) Four medieval gates (called bars) lead through walls built on Roman foundations to one of Europe's greatest medieval cities. You can walk round the top of creamy-coloured ramparts which surround the old city for 5km/3mi and protect a maze of winding, narrow streets (with ancient names like Stonegate and The Shambles) and medieval timber-framed houses.

At the heart of the city towers York Minster, the largest Gothic cathedral (built 1220–1470) north of the Alps. It is said that the beautiful windows hold more than half the medieval stained glass in England. A unique collection in the undercroft tells its story from Roman times to the present day. The city's history is also recreated visually and aurally in the Heritage Centre.

Other places of interest include the National Railway Museum; the 15th-century guildhall and Merchant Adventurer's Hall; 17th-century Treasurer's House; and the Castle Museum whose excellent folk collection includes reconstructed period houses and streets. More recreated atmosphere, plus original artefacts, are found in Jorvik Viking Centre.

Castle Howard, 22km/14mi NE, was the first creation of the English architect and dramatist, Sir John Vanbrugh. This magnificent 18th-century mansion, contains paintings by Rubens, Reynolds and Gainsborough. **Selby Abbey**, 21km/ 13mi S of York was founded in the 11th century by Benedictine monks; it has a Norman doorway and beautiful 14th-century stained-glass windows.

Isle of Man
The Isle of Man is about 48km/30mi long and 16km/10mi wide; its name derives from Manannan-Beg-y-Leir, reputed to be the first ruler. It is linked with Britain, and has the Queen as its monarch. However, it has its own Legislative Council (similar to the House of Lords at Westminster) and the House of Keys (similar to the House of Commons). These authorities pass the laws of the island, which are proclaimed annually at a ceremony on Tynwald Hill on old Midsummer Day (5 July). This is the oldest outdoor parliament in the world, and has its origins in the mode of administration used by the Scandinavians who once ruled here.

Douglas (pop. 21,100) is easily reached by regular sea service from Heysham.

The horse-drawn tramcars which ply the promenade are a distinct feature of this seaside resort; another is the famous tailless Manx cats in Nobles Park. Each June, the finest professional motorcyclists compete in the Tourist Trophy (TT) Race, while amateurs compete in the Manx Grand Prix in September.

Buses depart from the Central Bus Station, Douglas, to all main places on the island. Visit **Peel** (pop. 3081) on the opposite coast, 26km/16mi NW, famous for its Manx kippers and colourful sunsets. On nearby St Patrick's Isle, Peel Cathedral stands on the spot where St Patrick is said to have preached in AD 444. The castle has held such notable prisoners as the Earl of Warwick, locked up by Richard II after plotting against the Crown.

Laxey, 16km/10mi N of Douglas, is noted for remains of industrial archaeology, in particular the Big Wheel 'Lady Isabella', constructed to rid lead-mines of water. Laxey is the terminal for the electric Snaefell Mountain Railway which takes you to the summit of **Snaefell** (620m/2034ft) for panoramic views of England, Scotland, Wales and Ireland. Train enthusiasts will also enjoy the Manx Electric Railway (Douglas–Ramsey) and the Narrow Gauge Steam Railway (Douglas–Port Erin); both are over 100 years old.

Castletown (pop. 2820), once the Manx capital, is now a jolly resort, 24km/15mi SW of Douglas, guarded by Castle Rushen, one of Britain's best-preserved medieval fortresses.

The Isle of Man operates a seasonal trade and most hotels and guest houses close at the end of September, although larger resort hotels stay open, with limited accommodation, in winter. Book well ahead for summer. (See p. 15 for details of how to reach the island.)

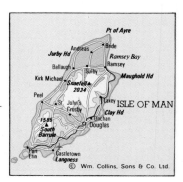

© Wm. Collins, Sons & Co. Ltd.

NORTH OF ENGLAND

For centuries the English–Scottish border was a no-man's-land, and in wilder days efforts to possess these 'Debatable Lands' often exploded in appalling battles and savage raids; today, the north is perhaps the most peaceful part of England.

The long ridge of hills called the Pennines divides the eastern and western parts, and it is these hills that give the character to the North Country way of life. The central position of the Pennines causes the hills to act as a watershed for many rivers; as these drain to east and west they serve all parts of northern England. Consequently great towns and cities grew up on the river banks and ports developed where they entered the sea.

The flavour of Pennine life can be found equally in a friendly country inn, at a lively open-air market, in a stone-built market town or among the grassy moors and dales. Throughout the region there are castles, priories, pele towers (fortified residences) and old abbeys to explore.

Towns on both sides of the English–Scottish border remember their stormy past in the Common Ridings – annual festivals in which local horsemen gallop over the moors and hillsides to 'beat the bounds'. Evidence of border warfare is also seen in the spectacular chain of castles built to defend the countryside and the long Northumberland coastline: dramatic red Bamburgh, gaunt craggy Dunstanburgh, impressive Alnwick.

The Lake District is England's largest National Park, containing the highest English peak (Scafell Pike) and Windermere, the largest lake. Throughout Lakeland there is climbing country and easier fell-side walks. To the north-east, in Kielder forest, lies the largest man-made reservoir in Europe.

Cumberland and Westmorland wrestling, probably the oldest Cumbrian sport, takes place at the annual sports in Grasmere, Ambleside and Coniston. Traditional fell-racing (to the top of the nearest hill and back) can also be seen at some of the Cumbrian sports meetings.

Several traditional Cumbrian crafts actively survive, and Kendal's Museum of Lakeland Life and Industry preserves those which haven't. Many craftsmen welcome visitors, and you can watch weaving in Grasmere, slate-working near Ambleside and leatherworking in Windermere (where you can buy rings made from local stone). Country industries thrive: a watermill still grinds flour for cakes and bread at Little Salkeld near Penrith; snuff is made in Kendal; clogs are fashioned at Whitehaven; pencils made at Keswick. Sweaters sold in Ambleside are made from the wool of local Herdwick sheep.

Mint Cake and Singing Hinnies Herdwick sheep also feature in local Cumbrian recipes, in the form of casseroled mutton. Other Cumbrian specialities include Westmorland Tatie Pot – a casserole of lamb, black pudding, pickled cabbage, potatoes and onions; Flookburgh Flukes – flat plaice-like local fish; and Cumberland sausage, which is flavoured with herbs and often several feet long.

The area is just as famous for cakes and sweets – try tasty Grasmere gingerbread and Cumberland Rum Nicky. Kendal Mint Cake (confectionery rather than cake) is made from sugar and was first devised to give energy to walkers and climbers. John Hunt's expedition took some up Everest to keep themselves going!

On the country's eastern side, the mixture of romance and firm practicality which characterizes this area is reflected in the local food. Filling and economical recipes using potatoes, leeks and leftovers are served in appetizing ways. Alnwick Stew and Pan Haggerty (cheese, onions and potatoes) are typical examples. Singing Hinnies, traditional scones cooked on a hot greased griddle until they sizzle or 'sing', are delicious when served warm.

Hotels, restaurants and inns throughout the area often have local dishes on the menu. Most main Lake District towns have a good market with stalls of jams, rum butter and mint cake as well as fish and meat. These include Carlisle, Cockermouth, Kendal, Penrith and Whitehaven. Local produce can also be bought in markets at Alnwick, Darlington, Hexham,

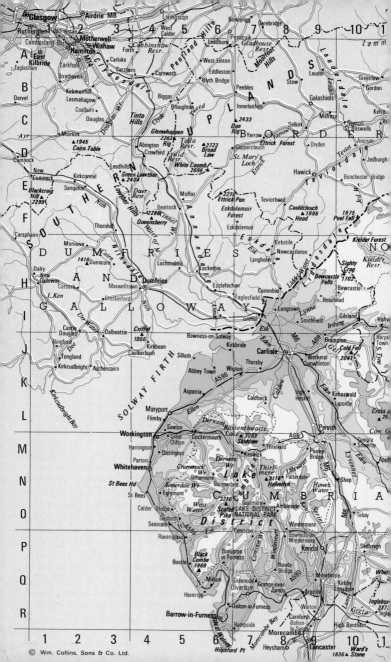

Newcastle and Stockton-on-Tees.

Festivals and Events Mid-April, Northumbrian Gathering – Morpeth; late April Teesdale Country Fair – Barnard Castle. I May, Riding of the Bounds – Berwick-upon-Tweed; early June, Appleby Horse Fair; mid-June, Durham Regatta; end June, Alnwick Fair. 4 July, Whalton Baal Fire Ceremony; early July Ambleside Rushbearing; mid-July, Durham Miners' Gala; Penrith Show. Early Aug., Ambleside Sports; Cockermouth Show; Grasmere Rushbearing; mid-Aug., Billingham International Folklore Festival; end Aug., Blanchland Show; Ennerdale Show; Grasmere Sports; Keswick Show; Patterdale Sheep Dog Trials. Early Sept., Kendal Gathering; Westmorland Show; end Sept., Egremont Crab Fair; Eskdale Show. Mid-Oct., Wasdale Show; Alwinton Border Shepherd's Show; end Oct., Wigton Horse Sale. 31 Dec., Allendale Baal Fire Festival.

Alnwick   E15
Northumberland (pop. 7190) The winding medieval streets of this Northumbrian market town have altered little over the centuries; Alnwick Castle, home of the Duke and Duchess of Northumberland, still dominates. This magnificent fortress dates back to the 11th century and, since 1308, when the Percy family took ownership, the castle has remained in the same family. It contains a fine armoury, keep and dungeon. The best time to visit Alnwick is on the last Sunday in June for the historic annual fair.

Craster, 10km/6mi NE, is a small fishing village famous for its oak-smoked kippers – herrings from the North Sea smoked in the traditional manner over fires of oak-chips. You can sample tasty results in the restaurant adjoining the curing-sheds. From Craster, an easy but dramatic 2km/1½mi coastal walk leads north to **Dunstanburgh Castle**, whose 14th-century ruins stand on cliffs 30m/100ft above the North Sea.

A few miles from Alnwick, the **Cheviot Hills** stretch north to the Scottish border. The Cheviots make up the northern third of the Northumberland National Park; their remote summits command inspiring views for miles around. The highest is Cheviot itself (815m/2676ft); it can be climbed in about two hours from Langleeford, south west of Wooler.

Ambleside and Grasmere   O8/O7
Cumbria Two of Lakeland's best-known towns lie within 8km/5mi of each other. **Ambleside** (pop. 2657), at the head of Windermere Lake, boasts one of the loveliest gardens in the area: **Stagshaw**, with its glorious azaleas and rhododendrons.

Grasmere (pop. 990) is internationally famous as the home of **Wordsworth** (Dove Cottage and nearby Rydal Mount are filled with the poet's memorabilia). As with Ambleside, there is a wide variety of accommodation and interesting specialist and craft shops.

Bamburgh   C16
Northumberland (pop. 458) According to Arthurian legend, Lancelot and Guinevere eloped to Bamburgh Castle; today it is used by film directors because of its dramatic setting high on a crag overlooking the sea. Inside, the hall and armoury with its large weapon collection are worth visiting.

Grace Darling is the heroine still revered in Bamburgh. She and her father, keeper of Longstone Lighthouse, Farne Islands, daringly rescued nine survivors from the wrecked S.S. *Forfarshire* in 1838. The Grace Darling Museum contains the rescue boat and various relics.

Seahouses 5km/3mi SE and **Beadnell** 8km/5mi SE are popular fishing resorts. From Seahouses you can take a boat-trip (April-Sept.) to the **Farne Islands**, sanctuary for seals and rare seabirds.

At **Beal** 19km/12mi NW, a 5km/3mi causeway connects **Holy Island** (also called **Lindisfarne**) with the mainland at low tide. Missionaries from Iona (Inner Hebrides) settled here in the 7th century, but were driven out by the Danes in 875. The ruins of 11th-century Lindisfarne Priory, which nurtured the growth of Christianity in the north of England, can be seen here along with Lindisfarne Castle, a 16th-century fortress restored in 1900 by the architect Sir Edwin Lutyens. There's also a mead factory where you can watch the process by which mead (an alcoholic drink based on honey) is produced.

Barnard Castle   N14
Durham (pop. 5270) The name of the castle christened the town, and this ruined 13th-century stronghold extends attractively along the banks of the River Tees at the town centre. Barnard Castle has connections with the writer **Charles Dickens**, and is a good centre for touring pretty Teesdale countryside.

The **Bowes Museum**, 5km/3mi SW, a splendid French-style château, houses a collection of internationally important fine and decorative arts, plus costumes, silver and English period rooms.

Raby Castle, 10km/6mi NE, the seat of Lord Barnard, dates mainly from the

Alnwick Castle, Northumberland

Durham Cathedral

14th century and shimmers romantically in its peaceful deer park.

Darlington, 24km/15mi E, is the home of North Road Station Museum, a collection devoted mainly to the Stockton–Darlington railway (the world's first steam passenger railway) which began life in 1825 transporting coal from pit-head to riverside. More 'railwayana' can be found, 11km/7mi N of Darlington, in the Timothy Hackworth Museum, Shildon.

Berwick-upon-Tweed   A14

Northumberland (pop. 11,647) Berwick is now England's most northerly town, but was once a great Scottish port and changed hands 13 times before finally becoming English territory in 1482. Berwick is a handy base for touring north Northumberland and Scottish Borderlands and is of great interest itself. The medieval town walls, reconstructed in Elizabethan times, are the best preserved in Europe. Take a breezy 3km/2mi stroll round the top for excellent views (guided walks usually available); also prowl around the quayside and see the three superb bridges spanning the Tweed Estuary.

Moving south west, **Ford** (19km/12mi) and **Etal** (16m/10mi) are both worth seeing. Ford is a picturesque model village recreated by Louisa, Marchioness of Waterford, in 1859. She spent 22 years painting the biblical scenes in the former village school (now Lady Waterford Hall), using local villagers for models. Heatherslaw Mill is one of England's oldest water-driven flour mills with its machinery still intact.

Carlisle   J8

Cumbria (pop. 71,582) Two thousand years of history, from the Roman occupation onwards, is indelibly implanted in the fabric of this old grey city. It was once the Roman camp, Luguvallium, the wall of which still runs north of the city. Other historical remains include Carlisle Castle with its 12th-century keep, 13th-century gatehouse and Museum of the Border Regiment containing trophies, weapons and medals.

Carlisle Cathedral, originally an Augustinian Priory, was made the seat of the Bishop of Carlisle in 1133. Today it is one of England's smallest medieval cathedrals and has a fine choir and presbytery with an exceptional medieval painted roof.

There's plenty of accommodation in Carlisle, so it is a good centre for discovering the unspoilt **Solway Coast**, designated an Area of Outstanding Natural Beauty. Here, the Irish Sea enters the broad estuary of the Solway Firth and England and Scotland are separated by 32km/20mi of water. Uncommercialized beaches and tiny villages like Allonby and Bowness-on-Solway typify this part of the coast, and you may be lucky enough to spot wild geese in flight.

Durham   K16

Durham (pop. 24,776) One of Britain's most visually exciting cities, with the vast Norman cathedral and castle rising above the city on their shared rocky hilltop. (Guided tours of both buildings are available.) The cathedral is an outstanding example of Romanesque architecture; among its treasures are the Galilee Chapel, resting-place of the Venerable Bede (a 7th-century scholar); church regalia and St Cuthbert's coffin are housed in the Treasury Museum. The University of Durham Museum of Oriental Art and the war relics in the Durham Light Infantry Museum are also worth seeing.

Hexham   I13

Northumberland (pop. 9270) This popular market town is well placed for exploring Hadrian's Wall and the Northumberland National Park. Thirteen hundred years ago, St Wilfred founded a church here which later became Hexham Abbey. Anglo-Saxon remains in the abbey include the crypt and Frith Stool – a sanctuary stool on which it is believed the Saxon kings of Northumbria were crowned. Other historic buildings include the 15th-century Moot Hall (council chamber) which is now an exhibition centre and the Manor House (now the Tourist Information Centre). The Hexham Music Festival is held in September and there's a colourful market every Tuesday.

Hadrian's Wall, the northernmost boundary of the Roman Empire, was built in AD 122 on instructions from the Emperor Hadrian; 168km/73mi of stone and turf snaked from Wallsend on the River Tyne westward to Bowness-on-Solway. Remains of barracks and military headquarters are visible at **Housesteads Fort**, 16km/10mi NW of Hexham. Vindolanda, 14km/9mi NW, has full-scale reconstructions of wall sections, and exhibits in the adjacent **Chesterholm Museum** include priceless Roman leatherwork, cloth and jewellery, preserved in almost mint condition. Roman remains can also be discovered at **Corbridge**, 5km/3mi E of Hexham, and at **Chesters** Camp and Museum, Chollerford, 8km/5mi N of Hexham.

Kendal   P9

Cumbria (pop. 21,596) Old grey limestone buildings lend charm and distinction to this peaceful Cumbrian town.

Ashness Bridge overlooking Derwentwater

Reminders of Kendal's long history include the 'yards' – defences set up for protection against purloining Scottish border raiders, and 12th-century Kendal Castle, home of Catherine Parr, Henry VIII's sixth, and last, wife.

The Museum of Lakeland Life and Industry is housed in the stable block of Abbot Hall, an 18th-century mansion with splendid period furniture. **Levens Hall** 10km/6mi S, is a Norman pele tower (fortified residence) converted to an Elizabethan mansion; the garden is famous for 17th-century topiary work.

Keswick   M7

Cumbria (pop. 5183) Set attractively among the Cumbrian Fells, Keswick has long been a centre for writers and poets. The Keswick Museum and Art Gallery contains manuscripts and relics of English writers such as William Wordsworth, Hugh Walpole and Robert Southey. Keswick is also the home of traditional rural events throughout the year, like the Agricultural Show in August.

Derwentwater, one of Cumbria's largest lakes (2km/1¼mi across), lies 1km/½mi SW. There are facilities for watersports and small boats for rent near Keswick. **Castlerigg Stone Circle**, 3km/2mi E, is a group of Bronze-Age standing stones.

The poet William Wordsworth was not the only famous son of **Cockermouth**, 18km/11mi NW. Fletcher Christian, chief mutineer on the *Bounty* and John Dalton, propounder of the Atomic Theory, had roots here. **Wordsworth House** was the poet's birthplace in 1770; it contains the original staircase, fireplace and panelling, and featured in *The Prelude*.

Newcastle upon Tyne   I16

Tyne and Wear (pop. 212,430) This regional capital is a busy commercial and industrial centre. Landmarks include St Nicholas Cathedral with its graceful lantern tower, the Norman Keep of the 'new' castle, and 15th-century Blackgate which houses the world's only Bagpipe Museum. Also visit the Hancock Museum (natural history) and Laing Art Gallery (British paintings). A traditional Sunday morning market is held on the historic quayside; Eldon Square, in contrast, is believed to be the largest covered city-centre shopping complex in Western Europe. Nightlife here includes friendly Northern nightclubs, old-time music hall and medieval banquets (details from Tourist Information Centres). **Washington Old Hall**, 10km/6mi SE, is the ancestral home of George Washington.

St Paul's Monastery at Jarrow, 11km/7mi E, is famous as the learning place of the Venerable Bede (673–735), a scholar and historian. The Saxon church and adjoining monastic remains are regarded as one of the most important early English Christian shrines.

Penrith   L9

Cumbria (pop. 10,590) This attractive red sandstone market town makes a useful touring centre for the flouncing countryside of the Eden Valley. Views from nearby Penrith Beacon (285m/937ft) extend to Scotland, while historical interest includes the ruined 14th-century castle built in defence against Scottish raiders.

From Penrith, you can easily reach **Lowther Wildlife Country Park**, 8km/5mi S, with its peacocks and wild boar; and the stone circle called **Long Meg and Her Daughters** 11km/7mi NE. A famous Horse Fair is held in June at **Appleby** 21km/13mi SE; Sulky Trotting Races (horse and carriage) take place on Bank holidays.

Whitehaven N4

Cumbria (pop. 27,600) Whitehaven has an appealing, faded charm. It was developed in the 17th and 18th centuries by the Lowther Family, and although the centre is being rebuilt, many of the original Georgian buildings have been retained, including St James's Church, the Friends Meeting House and the lighthouse. The port had strong American trading connections in the 18th century, and the Museum features local natural and industrial history with emphasis on the town's maritime past.

This part of the coast is rightly renowned for seabirds. **St Bees Head**, 5km/3mi SE, is a breeding-ground for guillemots and puffins, with more shore birds at Ravenglass.

The Ravenglass and Eskdale Railway starts its journey at **Ravenglass** 27km/16mi SE. Often called 'La'al Ratty', it climbs 11km/7mi from Ravenglass to Dalegarth, and was originally built to transport roofing slate from Eskdale to the coast for shipment. Now there are comfortable open and closed coaches and refreshments at both terminals.

At **Millom**, 51km/32mi SE, the Folk Museum contains interesting displays connected with the Hodbarrow Iron Ore Mines and Millom Iron Works, including a replica blacksmith's forge.

Windermere O8

Cumbria (pop. 7140) This popular Lake District resort, lying alongside England's largest lake, has plenty of accommodation and various watersport facilities. Sealink lake cruisers operate a regular sailing schedule between Bowness, Ambleside and Lakeside.

Take the ferry across Lake Windermere to **Grizedale Forest** where the visitor and wildlife centre (run by the Forestry Commission) includes observation hides, picnic sites, forest walks; 'Theatre in the Forest' presents classical music, jazz, drama and dance.

Troutbeck, near Windermere

SCOTLAND

Over the centuries, the rigours of the climate, poor natural resources and the long struggle for independence did much to shape the Scottish character; once you cross the Border, you'll notice a change both in accent and attitude. Scotland was never conquered; it joined the United Kingdom in 1707 by treaty, and even then retained separate legal and ecclesiastical systems. In architecture and landscape too it's a world away from England, and this sense of separateness is enhanced by the division within Scotland into lowland and highland, a split which is seen both geographically and in language and interests.

Lowlands

More rugged than parts of England, the Lowlands are a rich farming area (particularly sheep-rearing), yet also support nearly all of Scotland's industry and two-thirds of its population.

Separated from England by the Cheviot Hills, the Border country features a wealth of ruined abbeys at Melrose, Dryburgh, Jedburgh and Kelso, and abounds in tales of English-Scottish battles. History and folklore inspired the novels of Sir Walter Scott, who lived for many years at Abbotsford House near Melrose. Historical links are also strong in Lowland cities and towns like Dunfermline, an ancient capital, and Stirling with its famous castle, while east and west coasts sport popular seaside resorts and good golfing centres.

Edinburgh, with its 1000-year-old castle, is one of Europe's most beautiful capital cities. In the 18th and 19th centuries it blossomed as a cultural centre; among those who made names here were Sir Walter Scott, the poet Robert Burns, artist Sir Henry Raeburn, James Boswell (Dr Johnson's biographer), political economist Adam Smith and philosopher David Hume. Edinburgh's cosmopolitan air is sustained annually by its International Festival of Music and Drama. Only 72km/45mi away, the fine Victorian city of Glasgow forms the industrial heart of the Lowlands and is Britain's third largest city.

Highlands and Islands

The Highlands and Islands cover about a quarter of Britain's land surface, yet fewer than 1 in 50 of the population live here. The north-west area is mountainous and wild, with isolated moors and lochs (lakes), and stunning seascapes. This lonely landscape is Britain's last refuge for rare mammals and birds – golden eagles, wildcat, red deer. Winter skiing is enjoyed in the Cairngorm Mountains, particularly around Aviemore; another popular area of scenic splendour is The Trossachs in Perthshire. Attractions in the gentler, north-easterly part include ruined castles recalling the Middle Ages, and up-to-date whisky distilleries, some of which you can visit.

In the Outer Hebrides, the old Gaelic way of life survives in language, music and crafts. As well as the ancient Viking strongholds of Orkney and Shetland, there are many fascinating islands to see, from Islay with its whisky distilleries and Mull, haunt of red deer, to Iona where St Columba landed in 563 bringing Christianity to Scotland. Away from the main resorts, however, the number of shops, hotels and garages is limited and Sunday closing is observed in more isolated places. (The islands start on p. 121.)

Haggis and Whisky Next to Scotch whisky, haggis is probably Scotland's most famous speciality. It is made from a sheep's pluck (heart, lungs and liver) cooked, chopped and mixed with suet, toasted oatmeal and seasonings, then stuffed into the sheep's paunch, boiled and often served with Chappit Tatties (mashed potato) and Bashed Neeps (turnips).

Other dishes featuring vegetable mixtures include Clapshot (potatoes, turnips, chives) from Orkney, Stovies (potatoes, onions) and Rumbledethumps (potatoes, cabbage, onions) from the Borders.

Offerings from the sea and many lochs and rivers include fresh salmon (best from the Tay); Arbroath Smokies (haddock browned over oak-chip fires); Finnan Haddock, originally flavoured over peat fires at Findon, Aberdeenshire, and among kippers (salted, smoked herring)

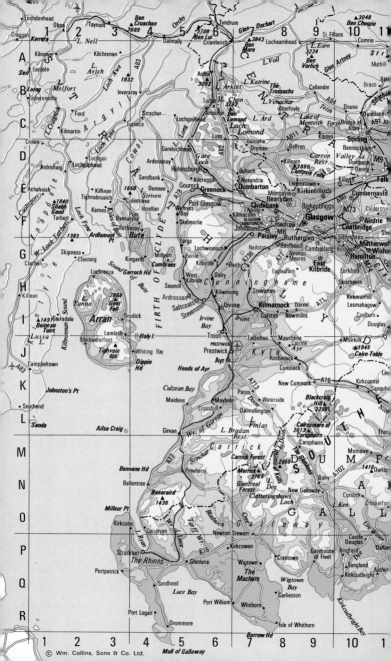

© Wm. Collins, Sons & Co. Ltd.

the Loch Fyne variety is especially tasty. Various fish soups have also evolved, like Cullen Skink (Finnan haddock, milk, onions, potatoes) from Grampian region and Partan Bree, based on crabs (partans) from Dumfries and Galloway. Other famous soups are Hotch Potch (mutton broth with vegetables), Cock-a-Leekie (fowl simmered with leeks) and Scotch Broth (thickened with vegetables and barley).

The Scottish sweet tooth is well known and shows itself in Butterscotch (a kind of toffee), Cranachan, a highland dessert using whisky, oatmeal, cream and sugar, Black Bun, a Festive cake rich in dried fruit, Dundee Cake, rich in fruit, peel and almonds, and Shortbread, a biscuit made with flour, butter and sugar.

Festivals and Events Jan., Up Helly Aa – Lerwick; Kirkwall Ba' Game; Burning of the Clavie – Burghead. Feb., Beef Shorthorn Cattle Show and Sale – Perth. March, Folk Festival – Edinburgh. June, Common Riding – Hawick and Lockerbie; Burns Festival – Kilmarnock; Guid Nychburris Festival – Dumfries; Royal Highland Agricultural Show – Ingliston; Braw Lads Gathering – Galashiels; Jethart Callants Festival – Jedburgh. July, Highland Games – Inverness; Mull Highland Games – Tobermory; Border Union Agricultural Show – Kelso; Plockton Regatta; Common Riding – Langholm. Aug., Ullapool Regatta; Highland Games in Perth, Crieff, Kinloch Rannoch, Nairn, Luss, Strathdon (Lonach Gathering); Edinburgh Military Tattoo, International Film Festival – Edinburgh; Edinburgh International Festival; Glenfinnan Highland Gathering; Cowal Highland Games – Dunoon; Birnam Highland Games – Dunkeld. Sept., Braemar Highland Gathering; Aboyne Highland Games; Langholm Agricultural Show.

THE LOWLANDS

Arran, Isle of   I3

Strathclyde (pop. 3576) The island of Arran is a miniature version of Scotland, with its own mountains, glens and lochs. Walkers are particularly attracted to uncultivated Glen Sannox to the north and Glen Rosa. The island is rich in history, with Bronze-Age cairns near Blackwaterfoot, on the west coast, and the King's Caves which sheltered Robert the Bruce in the 14th century. The view from the summit of Goat Fell (875m/2866ft) is one of the most extensive in Scotland. Brodick Castle, dating from the 14th century, contains an excellent art collection. Lamlash Bay and Whiting Bay are other popular holiday areas. (Details of how to get there are on p. 15.)

Ayr   J6

Strathclyde (pop. 47,896) Ayr lies at the heart of **Burns Country**, for it was at Alloway, 3km/2mi S, that Scotland's national poet was born on 25 January, 1759, a date celebrated by Scotsmen throughout the world as 'Burns Night'. His birthplace, Burns Cottage, is preserved as a museum. The Ayrshire landscape proved an inspiration for the poet, while places like Ayr, Kirkoswald (6km/4mi SW Maybole), Mauchline and Tarbolton (all with their own Burns Museums) are immortalized in his verse.

Ayr itself is an attractive resort with good beaches and a fishing harbour; its Tam O'Shanter Museum contains more Burns relics. North of Ayr you might visit **Kilmarnock**, 19km/12mi NE, centre of whisky-bottling, whose Burns Museum preserves numerous original manuscripts. South of Ayr, 18th-century **Culzean Castle**, set in a 200-hectare/500-acre Country Park, 14km/9mi SW, is one of Scotland's finest Adam houses; more fine architecture can be admired at ruined **Crossraguel Abbey**, 18km/11mi SW, a Cluniac monastery founded in 1244. **Turnberry**, 24km/15mi SW, is well known for its golf course.

Dumfries   N12

Dumfries and Galloway (pop. 29,382) Dumfries' best-loved inhabitant, the poet **Robert Burns**, lived here from 1791 until his death in 1796. His house in Burns Street (formerly Mill Street) is now a museum displaying personal mementos, while the Burns Mausoleum in St Michael's churchyard contains his tomb. Burns relics can also be seen at Dumfries Museum, the Globe Inn and The Hole in the Wa' Tavern, a commemorative statue stands outside Greyfriars Church.

Places to visit nearby include **Lincluden College** 1½km/1mi NW, originally the site of a Benedictine nunnery; **Maxwelton House** 24km/15mi NW, the birthplace of Annie Laurie, immortalized in the 18th-century love-song of the same name; **Ellisland Farm**, 8km/5mi NW, where Burns lived 1788–1791; Carlyle's House at Ecclefechan 21km/13mi E, a typical 18th-century Scottish artisan's house and birthplace of writer **Thomas Carlyle**; medieval **Caerlaverock Castle** 14km/9mi SE; Cistercian 13th-century **Sweetheart Abbey** at New Abbey 10km/6mi S; and **Gretna Green**, 35km/22mi SE, famous as the first place over the Scottish border where young runaway English lovers could marry in-

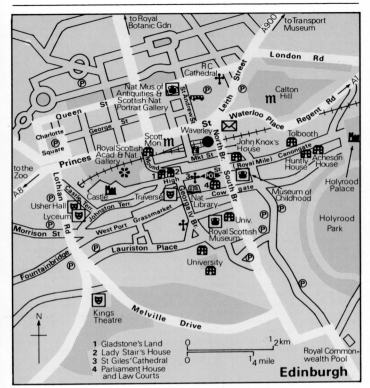

1 Gladstone's Land
2 Lady Stair's House
3 St Giles' Cathedral
4 Parliament House and Law Courts

0   1 2 km
0   1   4 mile

Royal Commonwealth Pool

Edinburgh

stantly without parental consent, until a law was passed, establishing a certain period of residency, which put paid to instant ceremonies.

Dunfermline   D13

Fife (pop. 49,897) This textile town was Scotland's capital for six centuries and several kings are buried here, including Robert the Bruce. As well as being the birthplace of the Stuart monarchs James I (1394) and Charles I (1600), the millionaire philanthropist, **Andrew Carnegie**, was born here in 1835 in a cottage preserved as a museum. Other collections to absorb are Dunfermline Museum (local history) and Pittencrieff House Museum (temporary exhibitions and costumes). The foundations of the original Dunfermline Abbey, founded in 1072 by Queen Margaret, wife of Malcolm III, lie beneath the present Norman nave. The 16th–17th-century town of **Culross**,

11km/7mi W, is splendidly preserved by the National Trust for Scotland.

East Neuk   B18/C17

Fife East Neuk is the collective name given to the fishing villages along Fife's easternmost coast. Narrow streets, picturesque cottages and tiny harbours characterize the villages of Crail, Anstruther, Pittenweem, St Monance and Elie. Once the haunt of smugglers, they are now more popular with artists and golfers.

Edinburgh   E15

Lothian (pop. 440,902) Edinburgh is more than Scotland's ecclesiastical and legal centre: it has the confident aura of one of Europe's great capitals.

The city commands a superb natural setting and was unique among Britain's ancient towns in the way it developed. The Flodden Wall, built in panic to guard the city after the English victory at Flodden, in 1513, limited expansion and buildings rose upwards not outwards. Rich and poor alike crowded together in a warren of tenements often ten floors high. In 1767, when Parliament approved the extension of the city, the New Town was conceived, blessing Edinburgh with a wealth of Georgian architecture. No. 7 Charlotte Square, furnished as a typical Georgian house, provides a handsome reflection of that age.

The oldest part of Edinburgh lies within the clifftop castle; St Margaret's Chapel dates partly from *ca*1100. Castle treasures include the Scottish Crown Jewels in the Royal Palace, 16th-century Great Hall, Scottish National War Memorial and Scottish United Services Museum. The floodlit Military Tattoo takes place on the Castle Esplanade during the three-week Edinburgh Festival (mid-Aug.–Sept.).

Many of the houses and 'wynds' (paths) date from the 17th century along the Royal Mile, which runs from the castle down to the Palace of Holyroodhouse, a 16th- and 17th-century Royal Palace with outstanding picture gallery and state apartments used by the Queen when in Edinburgh.

Treasures around the Royal Mile include: 17th-century Gladstone's Land in Lawnmarket and nearby Lady Stair's House containing literary mementos of Robert Burns, Sir Walter Scott and Robert Louis Stevenson. St Giles Cathedral, the High Kirk of Edinburgh, dominates the High Street. It was originally built in the 14th and 15th centuries; one particularly famous minister was the Calvinist John Knox. Behind St Giles, Parliament House was the meeting-place of Scottish Parliament from 1639 until the Act of Union in 1707. Just off High Street is the interesting Museum of Childhood and at the end of the street is 15th-century John Knox's House containing relics of the preacher who may have lived here from 1561–72. In the Canongate is 16th-century Huntly House, a local history museum, and opposite Canongate Church is 17th-century Acheson House, now the Scottish Craft Centre.

Princes Street, built on one side only, and named after George III's sons, brings the 20th century sharply into focus with its shops and gardens. Its principal architectural piece is the 60m/200ft Gothic spire of the Scott Monument (completed in 1844) commemorating the writer. Close by is the National Gallery of Scotland with a fine collection of Scottish, English and European masters. Other collections to see include the National Museum of Antiquities which shows the history and

everyday life of Scotland throughout the ages, and shares a building with the Scottish National Portrait Gallery; the Royal Scottish Museum where displays range from primitive art to space material; the Royal Botanic Garden, Transport Museum and Edinburgh Zoo.

Apart from its world-famous Festival of Music and Drama, Edinburgh provides a wide choice of year-round entertainment. Orchestras, bands and musical celebrities appear regularly at the Usher Hall. The Royal Lyceum and the King's present plays of a high standard and the Leith Theatre, with everything from pop to amateur opera, often presents children's shows. The Traverse Theatre Club produces experimental plays; temporary membership is available. There are many cinemas showing international films.

Glasgow   F9
Strathclyde (pop. 750,104) Traditionally, Glasgow was founded in the 6th century; by 1136 it had a cathedral and in 1451, a university. Commercial prosperity came in the 17th century with trade from the New World, and the city expanded again during the 19th-century Industrial Revolution with the nearby Lanarkshire coalfields providing power for the growing shipbuilding and engineering industries.

Architecturally, it is a Victorian city: look for City Chambers in George Square (Italian Renaissance style) and St Vincent Street Church (Greek and Egyptian style); a notable success was Charles Rennie Mackintosh's School of Art (1896). Glasgow Cathedral is the only complete example of pre-Reformation Gothic architecture on the Scottish mainland; it dates mainly from the 12th and 13th centuries. Nearby is Glasgow's oldest house, Provand's Lordship, built in 1471.

The marvellous Burrell Collection of paintings, furniture and objets d'art in Pollok Park, 8km/5mi SW of the city, has an astonishing range of over 8000 items. Glasgow also has one of Britain's best art collections in the Art Gallery and Museum, Kelvingrove Park, while domestic history is illustrated at the People's Palace. Other fascinating collections include the Transport Museum, the Hunterian Museum at the University (coins, books, paintings), and Haggs Castle, a special children's museum.

As for parks, there are plenty. On the north side of the river: Victoria Park, with its fossilized tree-stumps, the Botanic Gardens and Glasgow Green; on the south side: Pollok Park, in which stands the Burrell Collection and Pollok House, built in 1752 by William Adam, and containing fine paintings and furniture,

Loch Lomond

Rouken Glen, and Queen's Park.

The city is also the home of Scottish Opera and Ballet, both of whom perform at the Theatre Royal, while the Scottish National Orchestra gives concerts in the City Hall. One of Britain's best-known repertory companies is housed in the Citizens' Theatre. International cinema is presented at the Glasgow Film Theatre and the Third Eye Centre has art events and exhibitions.

Accommodation and transport make Glasgow the gateway to much scenic beauty: the Clyde coast, Burns country, the West Highlands, Loch Lomond and the Trossachs.

Hawick   K17

Borders (pop. 16,286) Hawick knitwear is exported the world over from this Border town and woollen-manufacturing centre; Wilton Lodge Museum contains exhibits related to this trade. The Horse Monument commemorates the town's youth who defeated an English raid at Hornshole in 1514; each June the event is recalled in the 'Common Riding', a gallop round Hawick's boundaries. Grim **Hermitage Castle**, 19km/12mi S, is the well-restored, 14th-century stronghold once owned by the Earl of Bothwell, Mary, Queen of Scots' third husband.

Jedburgh   J19

Borders (pop. 3893) Once the county town of Roxburghshire, Jedburgh is an excellent centre for riding, walking and climbing nearby hills and moors. Historic interest lies in ruined Jedburgh Abbey, one of the four famous border monasteries

founded by David I, and 12th-century Jedburgh castle, a property which frequently changed hands during Border warfare. Scottish Parliament demolished it in 1409, and the former county prison (built in 1823) stands on its site, now housing a small museum. Mary, Queen of Scots' House dates from the 16th century, and exhibits include her death-mask.

Kelso   I19

Borders (pop. 4852) This charming market town is a good base for touring the Cheviot Hills. Kelso Abbey (12th-century) was the greatest Border monastery until it was demolished in 1545. **Floors Castle**, seat of the Duke of Roxburghe, 1½km/1mi NW, was built by William Adam in 1721. Another Adam mansion (built by both brothers, William and Robert), **Mellerstain House**, lies 10km/6mi NW, and contains fine ceilings and period furniture. Other places of interest nearby include **Kirk Yetholm**, 11km/7mi SE, once the headquarters of the Scottish gypsies; and **Coldstream**, 13km/8mi NE, with its regimental museum. Coldstream was for centuries a focal point of border fighting, and an annual procession (Aug.) marches to **Flodden**, 5km/3mi E, bloody scene of the Scots' defeat in 1513.

Kirkcudbright   Q10

Dumfries and Galloway (pop. 2502) Kirkcudbright (meaning 'church of Cuthbert', and pronounced kir-coo-bry) is one of the most ancient towns in Scotland. The name, 'The Stewartry', used as an alternative when talking of Kirkcudbrightshire, recalls the past honour of being governed by hereditary Royal Stewards – an office held by the Maxwells from 1526 to 1747.

Kirkcudbright has attracted an active group of weavers, potters and painters; arts past are represented in 18th-century Broughton House, and folk items and natural history are displayed in the Stewartry Museum. MacLellan's Castle towers over the town, while another ruin, Tongland Abbey, lies to the north.

Kirkcudbright makes a good centre for exploring compact, mainly 18th-century Stewartry towns like **Castle Douglas**, 13km/8mi NE, close to Threave House with its colourful gardens. The island setting of Threave Castle can be reached by boat; this lonely 14th-century fortress was destroyed by Covenanters in 1640. **Dundrennan Abbey**, 8km/5mi SE, a ruined Cistercian house founded by David I, sheltered Mary, Queen of Scots, on her last night (16 May, 1568) in Scotland before she fled to England.

Loch Lomond C7

Strathclyde/Central This most beautiful inland loch whose 'bonnie banks' are celebrated in song, is the largest in Britain: 34km/21mi long by 8km/5mi at its widest point. Remote yet accessible, it is only 28km/18mi from Glasgow, and easily reached by train, bus or car.

The scenic softness of the southern area, dotted with islands, changes to mountainous grandeur at the northern tip. On the west bank the main road runs the length of the loch, the road on the east runs through Balmaha only to Rowardennan; there is a forest walk to Inversnaid, home of Rob Roy MacGregor. Ben Lomond (973m/3192ft), is an easy climb from Rowardennan.

The paddle steamer *Maid of the Loch* and many small pleasure craft, based in Balloch, sail in summer (mid-May–mid-Sept.) among the islands of the loch. There are Tourist Information Centres at Balloch and Tarbet.

Melrose I18

Borders (pop. 2185) This small town lies at the heart of Sir Walter Scott Country. Melrose Abbey, built for Cistercian monks by David I in 1136, was repeatedly destroyed during Border warfare and the ruins are mainly 15th-century reconstructions. The abbey was described by Scott in his poem *The Lay of the Last Minstrel*, and the heart of Robert the Bruce is said to be buried here.

Abbotsford House, Scott's home, stands 3km/2mi W. It contains mementos of the novelist and his study is preserved as he left it. Scott's grave lies amid ruined

12th-century **Dryburgh Abbey**, 5km/3mi SE; also buried here is Field Marshal Haig, the British Army's Commander-in-Chief in World War I.

Scott's favourite view (now called **Scott's View**) was from Bemersyde Hill, 5km/3mi E off the B6356, across the River Tweed towards the Eildon Hills. Another Border panorama can be enjoyed from **Smailholm Tower**, 11km/7mi NE off the B6404, a 16th-century keep featured in several books by Scott.

North Berwick D17

Lothian (pop. 4414) Golf, swimming, sailing and fishing are offered at this seaside resort, guarded by the 187m/613ft peak of Berwick Law, itself capped by a ruined watchtower. Another landmark is 106m/350ft high Bass Rock, teeming with seabirds and nesting gannets, in the Firth of Forth. Boats from North Berwick harbour provide trips round this and other island nature reserves.

Castles populate this coastline: **Tantallon Castle**, 5km/3mi E, the 14th-century stronghold of the Douglas family, was destroyed during the Civil War. **Dirleton Castle**, 5km/3mi SW, a 13th–16th-century fortress was besieged by Edward I in 1298 and ruined by Cromwell's troops; while the ruined castle at **Dunbar**, 13km/8mi SE, was Mary, Queen of Scots' retreat before her surrender to rebellious nobles in 1567. Dunbar is a popular resort, while inland, **Haddington**, 13km/8mi S, is a pleasant 18th-century town lying on the River Tyne.

Peebles H15

Borders (pop. 5884) This popular salmon-fishing centre is also noted for tweed and knitwear manufacturing. Among the town's historical pointers are ruined Cross Kirk, built by Alexander II in 1261, and the 15th-century bridge. Another 15th-century construction, **Neidpath Castle**, 1½km/1mi SW, was much battered in the Civil War but later restored. Even older is **Traquair House**, 10km/6mi SE, dating back to the 10th century; 27 English and Scottish monarchs stayed here – as well as Mary, Queen of Scots and Bonnie Prince Charlie. The house contains historical treasures and has a unique 18th-century brewhouse licensed to sell its own beer. Unlike Traquair, **Dawyck House**, 8km/5mi SW, is not open to visitors, although its impressive gardens are.

St Andrews A17

Fife (pop. 11,630) St Andrews is synonymous with **golf**; its Royal and Ancient Golf Club, founded in 1754, is the world's ruling authority on the game. The town has four coastal courses – the Old Course is the world's oldest, and a small fee will secure a game for you.

St Andrews also doubles as a popular seaside resort. Its university, founded in 1412, is Scotland's oldest; other historic buildings include the ruined 14th-century castle, complete with 7m/24ft deep dungeon. The 12th-century cathedral was once Scotland's largest church, although little of it remains today, and finds from the site, including Celtic and Medieval pieces, are housed in the museum.

Cupar, 14km/9mi W, is the market-place for a rich agricultural area and makes a good touring centre. At **Ceres**, 3km/2mi SE of Cupar, Highland Games are held each June to commemorate the villagers' safe return from Robert the Bruce's victory over Edward II at Bannockburn, in 1314. **Falkland Palace**, 13km/8mi SW of Cupar, was a hunting-lodge frequented by Stuart monarchs and has a 16th-century tennis court – the second oldest extant in Britain.

Stirling C10
Central (pop. 29,776) Gateway to the Highlands, Stirling is dominated by its majestic clifftop castle in which James III had the Parliament Hall built; James IV added the gatehouse and James V erected most of the royal palace (now containing the Museum of the Argyll and Sutherland Highlanders). Visit also the 15th-century Church of Holy Rude where Mary, Queen of Scots was crowned in 1543, the partly ruined Renaissance mansion, Mar's Wark, and the Landmark Centre which illustrates the castle's history.

Make pilgrimages to the **Wallace Monument** at Causewayhead, 3km/2mi NE, commemorating Scotland's medieval patriot, Sir William Wallace, and to **Bannockburn**, 5km/3mi S, the battlefield on which Robert the Bruce defeated the English army in 1314.

Stranraer P4
Dumfries and Galloway (pop. 9853) The pastoral scenery surrounding Stranraer, terminal of the 56km/35mi crossing from Larne in Northern Ireland, belies its turbulent history. Political and religious matters caused the bitter fighting marked by memorials to martyred Covenanters, 17th-century Presbyterian extremists, while ruined castles like Dunskey, near Portpatrick, recall Scotland's struggle for independence. In Stranraer itself, the 16th-century castle became the town jail, confining Covenanters in the late 17th century. Ruined **Glenluce Abbey**, a Cistercian house founded in 1192, lies 10km/6mi SE; further afield the scanty ruins of 12th-century **Whithorn Priory**, 29km/18mi SE, stand on the site of a monastery, Scotland's first Christian church, founded by St Ninian in AD 397. Several early Christian monuments, including the 5th-century Latinus Stone, are preserved in Whithorn Museum. At **Port Logan**, exotic plants flourish surprisingly in sheltered Logan Gardens, 11km/7mi S.

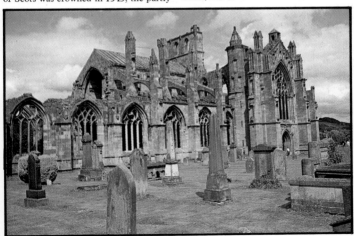

Melrose Abbey

THE HIGHLANDS

Aberdeen   I16

Grampian (pop. 214,100) Scotland's third largest city is built almost entirely from granite. Its recorded history dates from the 12th century, and old buildings include the Church of St Nicholas; 14th-century St Machar's Cathedral; 16th-century Provost (mayor) Ross's House, now housing the new Maritime Museum; 17th-century Provost Skene's House, restored as a local history museum. Other places to visit include Aberdeen Art Gallery and Museum (Scottish art); James Dun's House (museum); Cruickshank Botanic Gardens at Aberdeen University. The University itself combines two medieval colleges – King's (1494) in Old Aberdeen, and Marischal (1593) in the city. Fishing as well as North Sea oil contributes to Aberdeen's prosperity, but you have to rise early to enjoy the lively harbour fish-market: auctions take place around 0800. Aberdeen is noted for its sandy bathing beach.

Aviemore   I11

Highland (pop. 1000) This popular resort lies at the heart of Britain's main winter-sports area in the Spey Valley; a great attraction is the Aviemore Centre containing shops, cinema, theatre, and ice-rinks. To the east spread the Cairngorm Mountains, the major skiing-ground, and Glen More Forest Park, offering superb walks. Rare breeds – golden eagles, ptarmigan, deer and wildcat – inhabit the Cairngorm Nature Reserve.

The best months for skiing are February and March, although snow lies from November to May; summer skiing is possible around Cairn Gorm's 1245m/4084ft summit. Car-parks at 610m/2000ft offer access to chair-lifts while local restaurants include 'The Ptarmigan', Britain's highest at 1115m/3656ft. As well as at ski-schools and ski-shops, equipment can be rented at most hotels, which also provide après-ski entertainment. Other main Cairngorm centres are Kingussie and Newtonmore.

Braemar   J13

Grampian (pop. 1018) Braemar, famous for its Royal Highland Gathering (Sept.), is the nearest Deeside resort to the Cairngorm Mountains; other resorts are Ballater, Aboyne and Banchory. Visit 17th-century **Braemar Castle** and **Balmoral Castle**, 10km/6mi NE, a royal residence since Queen Victoria bought it in 1855. The grounds only are open to visitors when the royal family is not in residence; nearby Crathie Church is used by royalty. Over 150 castle sites are scattered between the mountains and the sea: most are around the salmon rivers of the Don and Dee; some are ruined, others still inhabited.

Callander   M10

Central (pop. 1768) This town is a useful centre for exploring the hills, forests and burns of Queen Elizabeth Forest Park and in particular the **Trossachs**, where you can take steamer trips in summer or walk and enjoy one of the most attractive areas in Scotland. The romantic appeal of this area was stimulated in the 19th century by Sir Walter Scott's novel *Rob Roy* and his poem *The Lady of the Lake*. The lake of the title was Loch Katrine, 14km/9mi long by 1½km/1mi wide, guarded by Ben Venue (730m/2393ft). At one time Callander's Kilmahog Woollen Mill was famous throughout the district for its handwoven blankets and tweeds; part of the old structure remains. The delightful village of **Brig O'Turk**, 10km/6mi W, has long attracted painters, including, in the 19th-century, Millais and the art critic Ruskin. **Doune Castle**, 11km/7mi SE, is one of Scotland's best-preserved 14th-century castles. In 1745 it was held for Bonnie Prince Charlie, and the hero of Scott's *Waverley* was imprisoned there.

Campbeltown   R7

Strathclyde (pop. 5960) Campbeltown is the chief town on the Kintyre peninsula. Its rocky beach provides good sport for fishermen, while golfers can enjoy Machrihanish's course. Sailing and sub-aqua are also available. Campbeltown Cross, an intricately carved Celtic cross, dating from 1500, stands at Old Quay Head. Beautiful gardens surround **Carradale House**, 21km/13mi NE, while at **Saddell**, 14km/9mi NE, there are remains of a 12th-century Cistercian monastery. **Mull of Kintyre**, the southern tip of the peninsula, is traditionally the landing-place of St Columba (521–97), who came from Ireland with his disciples to convert the Picts to Christianity.

Dornoch   E11

Highland (pop. 929) Situated on the sheltered shores of Dornoch Firth, this cathedral town has a famous golf course and a fair range of accommodation. Its 13th-century cathedral, severely burned in 1570, was later restored. Spectacular seascapes can be enjoyed all along this rocky coastline; other attractive resorts are **Brora**, 19km/12mi NE, and **Golspie**, 11km/7mi N, near which is **Dunrobin**

Castle, 13th-century seat of the earls of Sutherland. The house contains silver, furniture and paintings and has gardens laid out in 17th-century French style.

Dundee L14

Tayside (pop. 180,748) This old seaport and university city is noted particularly for jute production and its thriving jam-making industry, begun by Mrs Keiller who first made Dundee's famous marmalade in 1797.

Dundee was seized by the English in the 14th, 16th and 17th centuries, so few early buildings remain apart from 15th-century St Mary's Tower. The modern Tay road bridge (2km/1½mi) is the longest span over any river in the country. Places to visit include Dundee docks; City Museum and Art Gallery; Barrack Street Museum (natural history) and Mills Observatory. Claypotts Castle is a fine example of a late 16th-century fortified residence.

Glamis, 16km/10mi N, is famous as the site of **Glamis Castle**, ancestral home of the Earl of Strathmore, father of the Queen Mother. The 14th-century castle, largely rebuilt in the 17th century, contains fine furnishings. Shakespeare dubbed Macbeth the 'Thane of Glamis', although events in the play have no historical basis. The 17th-century Kirkwynd Cottages, in Glamis village, now house the **Angus Folk Museum** of agricultural and domestic life.

Elgin F13

Grampian (pop. 16,407) This bustling town makes an excellent centre for the Moray coast with its important fishing centres – Lossiemouth, Buckie, Macduff, Fraserburgh, Peterhead. Ruined Elgin Cathedral, founded in the 13th century, was one of Scotland's finest cathedrals; much of the original structure remains. Elgin Museum has a splendid fossil collection. Restoration of local ruined buildings include **Duffus Castle** 5km/3mi NW, and **Pluscarden Abbey**, 10km/6mi SW, originally founded in 1230, now reoccupied by Benedictine monks. Fortification of a different kind is provided by the **Glenfiddich Distillery** off A941 north of Dufftown (tours on weekdays only) or at **Glenfarclas Distillery**, 10km/6mi SW of Dufftown.

Apart from serving the distilleries, the River Spey is Scotland's third most important salmon river.

Fort Augustus I9

Highland (pop. 770) Fort Augustus commands the southern end of famous **Loch Ness**. Its former fort, named after Augustus, Duke of Cumberland, was built after the Jacobite uprising of 1715; the site is now occupied by a Benedictine abbey and school. Today Fort Augustus doubles as an angling centre and popular base for those tracking down Loch Ness's legendary monster. A more down-to-earth marvel is Thomas Telford's **Caledonian Canal**, a feat of 19th-century engineering, which links Lochs Linnhe, Lochy, Oich, Ness and the Moray Firth.

Fort William K8

Highland (pop. 4214) Fort William, at the foot of **Ben Nevis**, Britain's highest mountain (1344m/4408ft) is a touring centre for the Western Highlands. The fort itself was originally built in 1655 and named after William III, when rebuilt in 1690; it was dismantled in the middle of the 19th century. Bonnie Prince Charlie's 'secret portrait' is among the Jacobite relics in West Highland Museum. Ruined **Inverlochy Castle**, a 13th-century stronghold, lies 3km/2mi NE. **Glencoe** Visitor Centre, 16km/10mi S, illustrates events relating to the 1692 massacre of the Macdonald clan, due to their tardiness in forswearing the Jacobite cause. The **Glenfinnan Monument**, 28km/18mi W, erected in 1815, commemorates the Highlanders who followed Prince Charles Edward Stuart (Bonnie Prince Charlie) in 1745.

Gairloch F6

Highland (pop. 1783) Gairloch is beautifully set alongside Loch Gairloch among the wild and attractive scenery of the north-west Highlands. Good fishing and bathing facilities have encouraged its growth as a holiday centre. Inverewe Gardens at **Poolewe**, 6km/4mi NE, are remarkable for their subtropical plants; rare animals, including pine marten and wildcat, roam **Beinn Eighe** Nature Reserve, 22km/14mi SE, which has two nature trails starting from Loch Maree. Other villages with accommodation in this magnificently lonely landscape include Badachro, Port Henderson, South Erradale and Melvaig.

Inverness G10

Highland (pop. 57,526) Inverness is a useful centre for Black Isle, Moray coast and monster-hunting at Loch Ness. There's history as well as beautiful scenery: David I built the first stone castle here *ca*1141; however, all that remains of Cromwell's fort (1652–7) is the Clock Tower; 16th-century Abertarff House is now the home of the Highland Association, a body which ensures the longevity of Gaelic culture. Another highland pleasure is the regimental museum of the

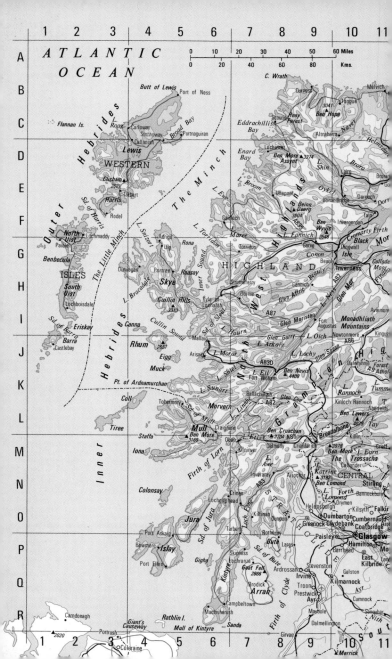

Pentland Firth

2 13 14 15 16 17 18 19 20 21 22

Mainland
Hoy St. Margaret's S. Ronaldsay
Hope
Duncansby Hd.
John O'Groats

Halkirk
Noss Head
Wick

Lybster

msdale

A
Herma Ness
Unst

B
South-haa Yell
Sullom Voe Brough Fetlar

C
Sandness SHETLAND
Mainland Whalsay

D
Scalloway Lerwick Noss
Foula Shetland Bressay
Islands

E
Mousa
Toab

F
Sumburgh Hd.

G
Fair Isle Same Scale

Lossiemouth
Cullen Portsoy Banff
Elgin Buckie
rres A98 Macduff Kinnaird's Hd.
Rothes Keith Fraserburgh
Spey Deveron Turriff Rattray Hd.
ntepn Dufftown A96 Huntly Ellon Peterhead
A95 Buchan Ness

H
N. Ronaldsay
Papa Westray
Westray Sanday

I
G R A M P I A N
Tomintoul Don Alford Inverurie
Ben Ahoyne Aberdeen Rousay ORKNEY
Braemar Dee Girdle Orkney Mainland Stronsay
Lochnagar K. Esk Banchory Ness Islands Shapinsay
3790 Stonehaven Stromness Kirkwall Skaill

J
Ballater
Kirriemuir Laurencekirk A92 Scapa Copinsay
ougowrie S. Esk Inverbervie Hoy Flow
Glamis Forfar Montrose St. Margaret's
I D E Brechin Hope S. Ronaldsay

K
Arbroath
Coupar Carnoustie Same Scale
Angus Sidlaw Hills Monifieth

L
New Scone Dundee
rth Firth of Tay
Tayport

M
Hills Cupar St. Andrews
FIFE Crail Fife Ness
inross Glenrothes

N
nbeath Buckhaven & Methil
Dunfermline Kirkcaldy
emouth Firth of Forth North Berwick N O R T H

O
Edinburgh Longniddry
Livingston Musselburgh Dalkeith Haddington Dunbar
gate LOTHIAN Prestonpans Cockburnspath St. Abb's Head

P
Penicuik Lammermuir Hills Eyemouth
ntland Hills West Duns Berwick-upon-Tweed S E A
Linton Greenlaw Holy I.
Peebles Moorfoot Galashiels Kelso Farne Islands
Hills Coldstream

Q
Tweed Melrose St Boswells Till Seahouses
Yarrow Selkirk Woolet Embleton
BORDERS Jedburgh The Cheviot Alnwick
Hawick 2676

R
Teviot Cheviot Hills Amble
Moffat Teviothead Otterburn Rothbury Coquet

2 13 14 15 16 17 18 19 20 21 22

© Wm. Collins, Sons & Co. Ltd.

Queen's Own Highlanders in 18th-century **Fort George**, 14km/9mi N. The oldest part of **Cawdor Castle**, 16km/10mi NE, is the 14th-century keep. The castle is surrounded by fine gardens and is associated with Shakespeare's *Macbeth*. The notorious Battle of **Culloden**, in which Bonnie Prince Charlie's forces were routed by the English, in 1746, is marked by a cairn on the battlefield, 6km/4mi E; a Visitor Centre explains the course of events.

Kyle of Lochalsh   H6

Highland (pop. 700) As well as being the main ferry-stage for the Isle of Skye, this bustling village is well positioned for touring the wild, scenic landscape around Glen Shiel, Kintail Forest, Applecross and Lochcarron, noted for its locally woven ties and tartans. **Balmacara** Visitor Centre, 5km/3mi E, is set in a magnificent mountainous stretch and offers walks, some guided, to Plockton Peninsula. Set in beautiful mountain scenery, facing Loch Duich, **Eilean Donan Castle**, 14km/9mi SE, was erected in 1220, rebuilt 1912. A 22km/14mi drive east from nearby Dornie brings you to the **Falls of Glomach**, among the highest in Britain, with a drop of 112m/370ft.

Oban   M7

Strathclyde (pop. 6897) Ferries run to the Western Isles from this busy port – to Mull, Coll, Tiree, Colonsay and the Outer Hebrides. Oban is dominated by McCaig's Folly, an incomplete copy of Rome's Colosseum, built as a family memorial by a local banker in 1890. Sailing, fishing, golf and swimming number among the pastimes offered to holidaymakers, while those in search of a little history might head for ruined 13th-century **Dunstaffnage Castle**, 5km/3mi N, where Flora Macdonald was imprisoned in 1746, or visit **Macdonald's Mill**, 1km/½mi S, to watch spinning and weaving demonstrations.

Perth   M12

Tayside (pop. 43,030) The 'Fair City' of Sir Walter Scott's novel, *The Fair Maid of Perth*, stands alongside the River Tay, Scotland's longest river, while the world-famous **Gleneagles** golf courses spread to the south west. Perth served as Scotland's capital until the court moved to Edinburgh, following James I's murder, in 1437. The Fair Maid's House dating from the 14th century, and home of Catherine Glover, the fair maid of Scott's novel, is now a Scottish crafts and antiques centre. In 1559 Calvinist John Knox delivered his notorious sermon on church idolatry from

St John's Kirk. Balhousie Castle, restored in the 17th and 18th centuries, contains the Black Watch Museum (Royal Highland Regiment), displaying medals, trophies, uniforms.

Scone Palace, 5km/3mi N, is famous as the coronation place of Scottish kings – the last was Charles II in 1651. Scone was the home of the Stone of Destiny until 1297 when Edward I removed it to Westminster Abbey. The present palace, largely rebuilt early in the 19th century, contains marvellous furniture, china and ivory and has extensive grounds.

Pitlochry   K12

Tayside (pop. 2599) A beautiful area of loch, river, mountains and woods surrounds this holiday resort. At Pitlochry Dam there's an observation chamber where springtime visitors can watch salmon leap upstream beside the hydroelectric power station (open to visitors). The town is also the home of Pitlochry Festival Theatre.

The **Tummel Forest Centre** at Queen's View, 8km/5mi NW, has interesting displays relating to the area; another visitor centre is at **Killiecrankie**, 5km/3mi NW, close to the battlefield where the Jacobite army routed King William's troops (1689). Castellated **Blair Castle**, 10km/6mi NW, the Duke of Atholl's home, contains antique furnishings, armour and interesting Jacobite relics.

Ullapool   E8

Highland (pop. 950) This old herring port is an excellent base for touring the wild, beautiful and lonely north-west Highlands. Ullapool is the main port for cruises to the **Summer Isles**, mostly uninhabited, and is also a prominent sea-angling centre. Here the streets are named in both Gaelic and English; local interest is found in Lochbroom Highland Museum. Ullapool is linked by ferry to Allt na h'Airbhe on Loch Broom's opposite shore. Pine marten, wildcat, deer and golden eagles hunt in **Inverpolly Nature Reserve**, 16km/10mi NE, while **Knockan**, 22km/14mi NE, is the start of an 80km/50mi nature trail passing through the Reserve.

Wick   B13

Highland (pop. 7842) The 19th century saw the enlargement of this old herring port. **Caithness Glass** is made at the modern glassworks where visitors are welcome to watch, and buy if they wish. Golfers are well catered for here, also those enjoying wild seascapes from the clifftop walks north and south.

The ruined 14th-century **Castle of Old Wick**, 1¼km/1mi S, is known affectionately to sailors as the 'Old Man of Wick'. More ruined castles stand in a dramatic setting 5km/3mi NE at Noss Head: **Girnigoe** is 15th-century and **Sinclair** dates from the early 16th century; both were abandoned *ca*1697.

THE ISLANDS

Inner Hebrides   F4/P4

Skye is perhaps the most famous of the islands with its history of Viking invasion, clan warfare and reprisals for harbouring Bonnie Prince Charlie when he fled from the English, aided by Flora Macdonald, after the Battle of Culloden in 1746. It also has the Cuillin Hills, spectacular landscapes and a strong Gaelic tradition. Places to visit include 13th-century Dunvegan Castle, home of the Macleod clan chiefs since 1200; Clan Donald Centre (gardens and museum) in 19th-century Gothic Armadale Castle, in the far south; Flora Macdonald Monument, Kilmuir churchyard and Skye Cottage Museum, Kilmuir, 32km/20mi NW of Portree. Accommodation details and guides from Skye Tourist Organization, Meall House, Portree (tel: Portree (0478) 2137).

Mull is beautiful, but wet, with lovely moorland, forest and peaks, the highest is Ben More (965m/3169ft). Close to Duart Point are 13th-century Duart Castle, stronghold of the clan Maclean, and Torosay Castle, Craignure, a mid-Victorian example of Scottish Baronial style. Calgary Castle gardens lie 16km/10mi SW of Tobermory. Theatre of Mull is one of the world's smallest. Tourist Information Centre (Apr.-Sept.), Tobermory (tel: Tobermory (0688) 2182). Accommodation lists for Mull, Coll, Tiree, Colonsay and local guides from Information Centre, Argyll Square, Oban (tel: Oban (0631) 63122 and 63551).

Iona, now owned by the National Trust for Scotland, is chiefly famous as the landing-place of St Columba, in 563, on his mission to bring Christianity to Scotland. The probable foundations of his cell on Tor Abb face the Abbey, which is well restored and dates back 800 years. Reilig Odhrain (cemetery) is the resting-place of sixty kings, including Duncan, murdered by Macbeth in 1040. Ten km/6mi away, the island of **Staffa** with cathedral-like Fingal's Cave, inspired Mendelssohn's Hebridean Overture.

Jura has a rugged terrain rising to the triple peaks of the Paps of Jura; the highest is Beinn an Oir, 783m/2571ft. It's a wild and empty island, haunt of red deer and refuge of rare plants (frosted orache, starry saxifrage). Peace and quiet and beautiful views are the main attractions. Consult Campbeltown Tourist Office (tel: Campbeltown (0586) 2056) for accommodation details.

Islay is the most fertile of the islands and offers good angling, fine beaches and several Celtic crosses, especially at Kildalton to the south and Kilchoman in the west. It has eight whisky distilleries; Bowmore's offers guided summer tours. Also visit Kilarrow Church, Bowmore, round and rare, built 1767, and Islay Folk Museum, Port Charlotte 18km/11mi SW of Bowmore. Tourist Office: (Apr.–Sept.) caravan in Bowmore (tel: Bowmore (0496 681) 254) or contact Campbeltown Tourist Office (tel: Campbeltown (0586) 52056) for accommodation details.

Ferry timetables from Tourist Offices or Caledonian MacBrayne Ltd, Ferry Terminal, Gourock (tel: Gourock (0475) 33755). Details of how to get there are on p. 14.

Outer Hebrides   B5/K1

The Western Isles are the last stronghold of Gaelic tradition and language, and Gaelic songs are still sung at ceilidhs (spontaneous gatherings). Lewis and Harris share the same island, with Harris occupying the southern quarter.

Lewis, a land of peat moors, lochs and sandy beaches, depends on fishing and weaving for its main industries. Stornoway, the capital, is a busy fishing port, sea-angling resort and centre of the Harris tweed industry. Sights here include 4000-year-old Standing Stones of Callanish; Carloway Broch, a Pictish tower; 16km/10mi NE of Carloway is the Black House Museum, Arnol, a traditional Hebridean dwelling. The Western Isles Tourist Organization operates five information centres round the islands. Headquarters is at 4 South Beach St., Stornoway, Isle of Lewis (tel: Stornoway (0851) 3088. It is open weekdays all year for accommodation details, ferry timetables and information on all the islands. Centres at Tarbert, Lochmaddy, Lochboisdale and Castlebay are seasonal (May–Oct.) and in winter enquiries should go to Stornoway.

Harris is more hilly than its neighbour Lewis, and the chief attractions are climbing and hill-walking. Harris Information Centre, Pier Rd, Tarbert (tel: Harris (0859) 2011). **North Uist**, with many prehistoric relics, **South Uist**, **Barra** and **Benbecula** are less visited by tourists so Sunday closing is rife. Tourist Offices: Lochmaddy, North Uist (tel: Lochmaddy (087 63) 321); Lochboisdale, South Uist (tel: Lochboisdale (087 84) 286). Details of how to get there are on p. 14.

Braemar Castle

Wildcat, Kincraig

Loch Maree

Eilean Donan

Cuillin Hills, Skye

Skara Brae, Orkney

Crail, Fife

Cawdor Castle

Oban

Orkney Islands   H22/L19

Lying about 32km/20mi to the north of the Scottish mainland, the Orkneys are made up of 67 islands, 30 of which are inhabited – the largest island by far is Mainland.

For 500 years Scandinavia ruled Orkney, and Norn (Old Norse) was the main language (*Orkneyinga Saga* relates Norse history in Orkney); legends about trows (trolls) and seal-maidens survive. Today Orkney shows achievement in the arts, as seen in the Pier Arts Centre in Stromness and St Magnus Festival of Arts at Kirkwall (June).

Orkney means 'seal islands' and you can see seals around **Sanday**. Seabirds are in profusion, especially at Marwick Head on Mainland, on **Copinsay**, **Westray** and **Papa Westray**. Wild flowers and hedgerow plants, rare in Britain, are also evident – oyster plants, orchids, alpines and the Scottish primrose, *primula scottica*.

Mainland offers much to see: Skara Brae, 11km/7mi N of Stromness, a well-preserved village built 4500 years ago; Maes Howe, 16km/10mi W of Kirkwall, a huge burial mound which may be Pictish; stone circles, Ring of Brodgar and Stones of Stenness, 8km/5mi NE of Stromness, impressive Bronze-Age monuments; Click Mill, 30km/19mi NW of Kirkwall, a primitive working watermill; The Brough of Birsay (a tidal island off the extreme north west) has a ruined Romanesque church.

In Kirkwall, the capital (pop. 4617), visit St Magnus Cathedral, founded 1137; ruined 13th-century Bishop's Palace and (adjacent) Earl's Palace, built (1607) for despotic ruler, Earl Patrick Stewart, and noted for Renaissance architecture; Tankerness House Museum. Buys include pottery, silverware and traditional Orkney Chairs; local tastes are Orkney fudge and Kirkwall kippers, and Highland Park Whisky Distillery offers guided tours.

Stromness, 24km/15mi W, where the ferry departs for Scrabster, grew in the 18th century with transatlantic trade; it has a good museum.

Flotta island is the North Sea oil terminal, and on **Hoy**, the Old Man (almost sheer and rising to 137m/450ft) is a supreme test for rock-climbers.

For accommodation, contact Orkney Tourist Information Office, Broad St., Kirkwall (tel: Kirkwall (0856) 2856). Details of how to get there are on p. 14.

Shetland Islands   A22/G19

On the northernmost fringe of the British Isles, the Shetlands lie 96km/60mi from the Orkneys and, like Orkney, the prin-cipal island is called Mainland. Only 17 of the hundred islands are inhabited.

Although more northerly than parts of Alaska, the Gulf Stream mellows the climate, and at midsummer, nights never become really dark: 'simmer dim' they call it. The original language was Norn, ancestor of Norwegian, which survived down to the 18th century; much remains in today's dialect. Cultural separateness is due to the islands' distance and Nordic ancestry – they only became Scottish in 1469 when Christian I of Denmark handed them over, with the Orkneys, to James III of Scotland in lieu of money pledged as his daughter's dowry.

Fair Isle, lying halfway between the Orkneys and Shetlands, is famous for its traditional knitwear and important bird migration observatory.

Mainland is the largest island and most southerly of the group. Fort Charlotte, built 1665, guards the harbour of the capital, Lerwick (pop. 6127), from which ferries run to Aberdeen. Up Helly Aa, a Viking fire festival, is held in Lerwick at the end of January. Sights to visit include Jarlshof Prehistoric Site at Sumburgh, near the airport; Mousa Broch, a well-preserved Pictish tower reached by boat from Leebotten 20km/12mi S of Lerwick; Tingwall Agricultural Museum, north of Scalloway; Croft Museum at South Voe, Boddam 40km/24mi S of Lerwick; Scalloway Castle built *ca*1600 by the tyrannous Earl Patrick Stewart, nephew of Mary, Queen of Scots, who ruled both Orkney and Shetland at the end of the 16th century. Sullom Voe, the vast oil terminal, is not open to visitors but it is worth driving up B9076 to see the area.

Of special interest: Shetland ponies (on **Fetlar** and **Unst** islands); traditional woollens and silvercraft; excellent bird watching, particularly at Herma Ness on Unst (razorbills, fulmars), Staffaberg on Fetlar (skuas), Isle of Noss (gannets, eiderduck); seals around Herma Ness and Mousa and otters around Fetlar, **Yell** and Unst; wild flowers in spring and summer (ragged robin, hayrattles, orchids).

For accommodation, contact Shetland Tourist Organization, Market Cross, Lerwick (tel: Lerwick (0595) 3434). Details of how to get there are on p. 14.

INDEX

All main entries are printed in heavy type. Map references are also printed in heavy type. The map page number precedes the grid reference.